I'VE GOT A POLE YOU CAN CLIMB

Tales of a Telephone Technician

Shelley Staib & Christopher Gulick

While the stories in this collection are true, the names of most of the people represented have been changed, altered, or varied enough so that they will have to guess if it is them. Any resemblance to anyone is purely coincidental. Whatever ...

Published in the United States by HARD-SHORT Press, LLC.

Cover Art: Moon Ultracool aka Matthew Staib
Interior Illustrations: Graeham Jarvis
Forward & Story Selection: H.B. Berlow
Editing: Kelsie Baab
Consultant: Sara Lamb

ISBN: 1732501106
ISBN-13: 978-1-7325011-0-2

FORWARD

"Once upon a time ..."

It's a phrase that usually starts most fairy tales. Given the fact that there is an entire generation who has NEVER HAD a landline, I guess these stories of telephone technicians are like fairy tales.

Now, we're not going to get into the technology behind wireless service and how it actually DOES connect, at some point, somewhere, to a wire. These stories are not about technology. They're about people in the workplace dealing with real human beings. And animals.

From 1997 to 2010, I was employed by Southwestern Bell (which then became SBC which then became AT&T, or more correctly, returned to being AT&T). I was in the Business Office, a term that you would think implies Customer Service but in actuality meant Sales. Where I worked, you sold stuff. Products. Services. Stuff.

If you had a heart, you probably didn't sell much because you were too busy caring about people. In that case, your supervisors were scrutinizing you more closely, finding ways of thinning the herd.

So, I dealt with sweet but nefarious supervisors and customers. (No animals.) But I dealt with them strictly over the phone where the MUTE button became a useful tool, despite the fact that the supervisors discouraged you from using the MUTE button because they claimed it didn't always work, which says a hell of a lot for the rest of their technology.

(As you are beginning to realize, this is one of the primary reasons I write crime fiction. You can't ACTUALLY do away with customers, but they DO make excellent victims in your novels.)

The Customer Services Technician (what most folks referred to as a Repairman) dealt with all the known human deviations live, face-to-face, in all kinds of weather. The fact that anyone who had a landline could pick up a phone and hear a dial tone was a testament to their skills. It got to a point where customers expected everything to work. All the time.

Perhaps the company is efficient to a fault. Often, rather than being praised for their efforts, the Customer Services Technicians encountered a variety of individuals who were technologically challenged on the one hand but on the other were rather adept at all of George Carlin's "Seven Words You Can't Say on Television."

Well, guess what? Things break. That's where people like Shelley and Chris came in. With over 60 years of experience between them, suffice it to say they knew their shit. But, as previously stated, this is not about the technology. This is about people working for a living and facing the strange and unique and heartwarming and touching and just downright weird.

Nowadays, jobs are in offices, in cubicles, with computer screens and cell phones or tablets lying on the desk nearby. Sure, we get together at lunch … maybe.

The world of retail shopping is giving way to the online experience. Even grandma can do her Christmas shopping on Amazon and not have to worry about traffic. There are hardly any jobs today in which people deal directly with other people.

We can't tell what the future holds, but we can look back upon the not-too-distant past when the World's Largest

Telecommunications Company provided amazing products and services and had the best-qualified technicians to keep everything working.

These stories are from the workplace. They involve real people. This is the kind of stuff that you can't make up. It has to be lived.

And Shelley and Chris lived through it all.

H.B. Berlow

Author of *Ark City Confidential*

CONTENTS

THE NON-INTRO INTRODUCTION

There is no introduction chapter because most people don't read that part of a book. I sure as hell don't. You see, I am a technician. As the saying goes, "I don't need no stinking instructions!"

The first thing out of the box and onto the floor is, you guessed it, the instructions. That sheet is referred to only during the course of working on something when it becomes obvious some damned engineer decided that something that works well needed a tad bit of messing with, like, oh, the laws of physics.

Male or female, does not matter. True technicians have a natural mechanical aptitude that enables us to intuitively understand that which baffles most of you members of the general public. I'm not bragging; that's just how it is.

For instance, I am not a school teacher. There is a good reason for this. I would attempt to fix or repair your little brat, or even better, YOU.

All technicians go back to the point of origin of the trouble. This is why I would start at the conception of your ancestors and begin the repair work there. You now know why I do what I do. Natural selection.

Okay, back to this chapter and the lack of a section called the introduction. I'm troubleshooting the reader's tendency to skip the introduction. Yes, psyching you out. These stories, as well as the glossary, contain information you will need to understand (to some kindergarten degree), techie terms about phone service and the parts and equipment that make it possible for you to discuss all-important subjects like your ex-husband's slut girlfriend, the party you don't remember, or your latest 18-hour surgery.

So ... pay attention and refer back to this chapter and the glossary often to remember simple stuff you already forgot.

By the way, if you are already offended, then you are one of the moronic customers that we will be referring to on countless occasions throughout this text. Either throw this book away now or schedule a counseling session to learn how to not take yourself so seriously. You will then thoroughly enjoy the upcoming stories.

BTW, it does not matter if we're a woman, man, straight, gay, brown, black, other, Buddhist, Baptist, or the odd person living next door to you. Nor is it important if we currently work for or previously worked for an independent company or one of the big "Corps."

None of those things matter.

ALL THESE STORIES ARE TRUE!

I promise you; no one could make this stuff up.

Most of these stories are ours. Some of them are stories passed along by fellow technicians. Only the names and places have been changed to protect the guilty.

Some of these stories might be about YOU. But, hey, don't flatter yourself or get all indignant. It happened somewhere else as well. None of these are really all that unique.

Weird, funny, sad or just plain stupid. But unique?

Nah.

A WOMAN'S PERSPECTIVE

Sometime in the seventies, the telephone company was court-ordered to hire women and people of color for outside service technician positions. Up until that point those positions were filled by white guys. I was 18 years old in 1975, had just graduated from high school and had no idea what I wanted to do. An uncle of mine was a mid-level manager at Ma Bell, and he suggested I apply for a job as an installer. So, I did. All I knew was I would get to work outside, and that the money was good. I was hired along with 12 other women–it wasn't until later I learned that there were only 6 open positions in the city. What that said to me was that at least 50% of us were expected to fail at some point in the training. The first thing we had to do was learn how to climb a telephone pole. If we can't pass that part of the training, we couldn't be an installer/repair technician. If we made it through pole climbing, the next course was basic electricity. The training facility was in another city. It was December; it was cold and the pole climbing yard was outside. The group ahead of us had completed their pole climbing training, and I was asking one of the men in that group what it was like.

"Well, I guess you heard about what happened," he said cautiously.

"No. What are you talking about?"

"Oh my god, the instructors didn't say anything to you yet? One of the women in our class fell off the pole backwards, broke her neck, and died."

My jaw dropped. Maybe this was a bad idea. Maybe pole climbing was not something I needed to learn. Maybe that's why I kept seeing an ambulance circle the block every hour like clockwork. Turns out the woman was taking a prescription painkiller, which she had not disclosed to the instructors. It also turns out she was supposed to have belted on. That is when your climbing belt is secured around the pole - but she hadn't. She climbed to the height she was instructed to climb to and then simply leaned back, free falling about 25 feet to the ground.

Talk about an inauspicious beginning.

An investigation was underway, and both instructors were understandably shaken up. Once I knew what had happened, I was less fearful and even more determined to be successful. Let me say here that Ma Bell *always* placed safety first. We were taught and trained how to do our job safely and to trust our equipment as long as it was being used properly. After 40 years, I still remember the safety motto: "No job is so important, and no service is so urgent that we cannot take the time to perform our work safely." This was drilled into our heads from day one and for good reason. When working aloft on a pole at twenty-five feet in the air, wearing a pair of climbing hooks strapped to your calves, standing on a couple of sharpened steel points that went into the pole less than an inch, leaning back against the safety belt so as to be able to work freely with your hands–yeah, you wanted to be able to trust your equipment and have confidence in everything you're doing. One of the ways to build that confidence was to have new trainees throw a basketball to each other while belted on at about 20 feet. Now me, I was a tomboy who played sports growing up so throwing a basketball while up on a pole sounded like fun. Until the instructors added this caveat: anytime someone dropped the ball the entire class had to climb down and climb back up again. About the sixth time we did this, I was starting to get irritated. Thoughts like, "I threw that ball directly into your chest how the HELL did you not catch that?" and "Who paints their fingernails to go to pole climbing school?" were running through my head. I will say, however, I felt pretty damn comfortable up there, and I knew as long as I climbed the way they taught me to climb, I would be okay. I would be safe.

Ultimately, I passed pole climbing and basic electricity and installation school. The real training was just beginning: moving from the classroom to the field.

Being one of the first women to fill this position was both exciting and challenging. I was fortunate that most of the men I worked with were open-minded about women doing this kind of work. There were a few holdouts, and they made it clear they weren't happy with my being there. I knew I could do this job, and I meant to prove it to them. In fact, as time went on and other women followed in my footsteps, I would do everything I could to help them be successful, but at the same time, I was probably harder on them than the guys. I worked my ass off to prove I could do this job, so do not come in here and ask one of the guys for help carrying your 60-pound ladder. Truthfully, not many women stayed in this job once they tried it. They either moved on to another, less physically demanding job or they left the company.

One of the things that surprised me was the reaction of female customers when I showed up at their door. I think I expected some people to be wary or at least curious (and a lot of them were), but I was taken aback when a female customer would look over my shoulder and say, "Where's the phone man?" Hey, nobody said being a trailblazer would be easy, but show a little solidarity, sister! I had customers follow me around the entire time I was working, asking things like, "Are you sure you know what you're doing?" and "How does your husband feel about you doing this type of work?" And one of my favorites: "Doesn't it bother you that you're taking a job away from a man with a family to feed?"

Yes, I know what I'm doing; you wouldn't ask that of a man.

I'm making more money than my husband; he doesn't mind. (I am not married, not that it's any of your business.)

I have three kids I have to feed. (Nope, I don't.)

Clearly, I thought lying was okay in the face of presumptuousness.

On the other hand, some people were so amazingly supportive, it was heartwarming. There were many times when my customers would be delighted to see a female technician was there to do the work, and most of them were curious and asked lots of appropriate questions. I received questions like, "What made you decide to be a technician?" and, "Is it scary to climb a telephone pole?" and "Do people think it's weird when a woman shows up to do the work?"

People are curious by nature, and I never minded answering questions that were not asked in what I perceived to be a condescending manner. I realized that I was breaking new ground, so I expected some pushback, maybe some resistance. It took time to establish myself, but the men I worked with and the customers themselves saw that I was both willing and capable of doing what this job required.

Customer service was a hallmark of the telephone company, and I prided myself on leaving the customer with a better impression when

I left than they had prior to my being there. On those occasions when I couldn't fix the trouble or complete the installation for whatever reason, it was important to me that the customer knew I had given it 100% and that their service request would be taken care of by the department I handed it off to.

In the first year or two, I know I worked even harder to prove I could do this work, and I earned the respect of my fellow technicians as time went on. Being one of just a handful of women who began and ended their careers in an outside technician position is a source of tremendous pride for me. I loved working outside, going into people's homes and businesses, troubleshooting the problem, and finding a solution. My phone truck became, quite literally, my second home.

There were months and years when I spent more time working than anything else. I remember doing my laundry at midnight because that's the only time I had to do it. Many times, I'd made plans for that evening or that weekend only to have to cancel them at the last minute because of the demands of the job.

One thing I am very grateful for is being paid equal wages. I made the same amount of money as the men I worked with. There was complete equality from my first day until the day I retired. It saddens and angers me that even now that is not the case in many workplaces. I'm proud that the telephone company, in partnership with the Union, was at the forefront of equal wages for women.

To be honest, I didn't really understand how fortunate I was initially. I was eighteen years old, and I'd had a total of two jobs in my young life up to this point. I worked at a popular drive-in while in high school, and then I worked for a new apartment complex doing maintenance and landscaping for a few months while I waited to see if my application was accepted. Once I started paying attention, I realized how much women were, and are, discriminated against as far as pay goes. Because of the Union, I received good wages and, as my career continued, I made more money than a lot of my friends with college degrees.

I worked a lot of overtime, as much overtime as I wanted, and often more. When we were in a service emergency—which typically followed Mother Nature's wreaking havoc with ice storms, torrential rains, high winds, tornadoes, snowstorms, and lightning strikes—we worked seven days a week, twelve hours a day, if not more. This made for some great paychecks. But when you are working that much, after ten days or so, you go into this automaton state of mind. You have to be careful because when you're twenty-five feet up on a pole, you need to be alert and present, and that's not always the case when you've already worked sixty hours and the week is not yet over.

Ultimately, my safety was my responsibility, and it was also up to me to find a balance between my work and my personal life. That was not something that was easily done and, in fact, it took many years for me to learn how to do so. I used to listen to the guys on my crew talk about how much overtime they worked. There was usually a competition between some of them to see who worked the most hours in a pay period. They would complain that they had to mow the yard last night when they got home at eight thirty in the evening. I would respond with something like, "And did your wife cook your dinner for you and do your laundry? Yes? And she cleans the house, too? Wow! Because I worked as many hours as you did, and I cooked dinner, did the laundry, cleaned the house, AND mowed the yard." Just saying.

ADVENTURES IN CLIMBING

It's been forty years since I learned to climb telephone poles, and I still get a kick out of telling someone that's one of the many things I did as a technician. That still gets someone's attention right off the bat, even today.

There were three ways to climb a pole, generally speaking. You could hook it—using the leg irons strapped to your calves, sinking the half inch or so of sharpened steel into the side of the pole with each step up. Or if it was a stepped pole, it had metal 'steps' (about six to eight inches long) driven perpendicular into the pole which you used as both a handhold and to stand on. Or you could use your ladder and which way you climbed depended on many variables, safety being the priority and access being the next factor. As in, how the hell am I going to get to the pole, much less climb it?

I will tell you that there is a thrill to it, climbing up on a pole and belting on up there. Twenty or twenty-five feet in the air. I loved it, especially working out in the country. I'm up there on a gorgeous day, surrounded by wheat fields gently undulating in the wind. The sky is clear, and it seems like I can see forever looking out at the horizon. It's a view not everyone gets to see in their work, and this is my office.

I remember the first time I was on a pole and there was a storm. It was moving in quickly, this being Kansas. It was beautiful to watch from up there. I could see it gathering in the distance, wisps of clouds swirling white against the darker clouds in the background. I had just a few more minutes of work to do up there and I would be done with the aerial part of this job. I am remembering everything I was taught about not being on a pole when there's lightning. Then I see, off in the distance, lightning strike. I raise my hands and lean back against my belt and remember that lightning can travel many miles in an instant. OK, I'm done. I start my descent, my heart is pounding, and I just want my feet back on the ground.

Beautiful and, in the blink of an eye, dangerous.

Oh, the things that happened at about 25 feet in the air ... wasps, for example. They loved building their nests inside our terminals where we hooked up aerial lines for service to people's houses. Let me help you picture what it looks like the first time you find a wasp nest. You're on a pole; you're belted in so you can lean in as close as you need to or lean back maybe three feet, give or take. Three feet at the most between your face and the angry mob of wasps that attack you when you open up the terminal and expose their nest and all the eggs. I am speaking from experience, as you know, when I say it was like a scene from one of the 1940's era war movies, where the wasps looked like a squadron of Japanese kamikaze planes, dive bombing and dodging and deadly in their relentless attack!

I let loose with, "FUCK YOU, LITTLE MOTHERFUCKERS," waving my right arm, trying to knock them away while reaching in my canvas bag for the can of Wasp Killer someone told me to always carry in the spring and summer months. Now I know why! I'll have it ready before I open the terminal next time, but now I aim it at the nest and saturate

10

it, killing the wasps instantly.

I don't have to wait for long when I hear a couple of them buzz around my head, and I take aim again and knock a few more down in the air. This spray we use shoots a solid stream of poison about twenty feet—it's quite a lot of pressure, and it paralyzes the wasps and kills them instantly. I am only stung twice, and it hurts like hell, but I feel lucky it isn't worse. I hope nobody heard me shouting profanities. I must have looked like a crazy woman up there! Now that I'm no longer under siege, I can complete my work.

There were many times when I'd be up on a pole and people wouldn't know I was up there. I saw some interesting things from up there, you know, like women sunbathing topless in what they believed to be the privacy of their backyard. This didn't happen a whole lot, but it did happen occasionally. Talk about an awkward situation. I've climbed up and belted on; I'm looking around up there when I notice this woman, in the yard next door, sunning herself by her pool. Now, I certainly don't want to call attention to myself, so I would just get my work done as quickly and quietly as possible and hopefully get down without anyone knowing I was ever up there. That's just me. I'm pretty sure most of the guys I worked with would have taken their sweet time. They'd have probably gotten sunburnt from being up there so long.

Another odd phenomenon occurred when I worked in the downtown area where the outreach services are located for the homeless. Invariably, if I was on a pole, I would see one of the homeless population using the alley as a toilet. Men and women, it was an equal opportunity alley. Unisex. No one had to worry about leaving the lid up in this situation.

Then there were times when I had to get to a certain pole to do some work, but the pole was in someone else's yard. This person would not be expecting me, and, more often than not, would not be home - which was fine because then I didn't have to explain what I was doing and why I needed into their backyard. However, this sometimes backfired.

Case in point: the pole I needed to climb was in a yard that had a six-foot privacy fence. I rattled the gate and whistled; if there was a dog back there, I wanted to get his attention before I let myself inside the yard. There was no lock on the gate, and no dogs were out, so I cautiously stepped into the yard. I saw evidence of a dog though—a doghouse and some toys scattered about, a water dish and food bowl on the patio. I closed the gate behind me and climbed the pole. I was up there about fifteen minutes, on the phone with our test center, when I heard barking from inside the house and then the sliding door opened, and the dog raced into the backyard, making a beeline straight for the pole.

It was a male Rottweiler and he was beautiful. He planted himself at the bottom of the pole, barking steadily as if saying, "Come on down. I dare you." I wrapped it up with the test center and then connected my headset to the customer's line whose yard I was in. I dialed a special number which reads back that customer's telephone number, then I hooked up to a different number and called the Rottweiler's owner from the pole.

"Hello?" a woman's voice answers.

"Hi, my name is Shelley and that's my phone truck parked in the street in front of your house. I'm actually up on the pole in your backyard, and I was wondering if you'd call your dog in the house, so I can climb down?"

"You're where? In my backyard?" I can hear the confusion in her voice.

"Yes, ma'am. Up on the pole. If you look out your sliding door, you'll see me. There you are–hi!" and she smiles as she makes eye contact and waves. As soon as she calls the dog, he trots back to her and goes inside the house. I close up the terminal and climb down, spend a few minutes explaining what it is I'm doing and then thank her for her time and leave. It doesn't always work out so nicely.

Once, I was called out to help one of the guys on my crew. Help may not be the right word—it was more like a civil standby, where I provided support for him on this job. All Paul says on the phone is, "This lady is a real piece of work. You'll see when you get out here."

This is another instance of needing to gain access to the pole that is in this woman's backyard. We are not working on her line, but one of her neighbor's. Since we aren't working on her line specifically, she refuses to let us in the backyard. I pull up behind Paul's truck, and he gets out to talk to me.

"She isn't budging. She will not let me in the damn yard! I think I can get to it through the yard behind, though. Follow me over there."

We drive around the block and there is a narrow access to the pole between two fences of the adjoining properties. It's a tight squeeze just walking through, and Paul must get a ladder back there as well as get up over the fence on this side. It would have been so much easier from the other yard. Paul gets the ladder positioned and begins ascending. I watch from a few feet away as he is calling the test center. He looks over at me and says "I'm on hold. Shocking surprise." He shakes his head and thanks me for coming out. At that moment, we both hear the hounds of hell being unleashed.

I can see into the backyard where the pole is, and there are three pit bulls flying across the dirt-packed yard, all muscle and jaws and bared teeth, heading straight for Paul, who is watching from relative safety twenty feet up. I say relative because they are jumping up and down like spring-loaded machines, their mouths starting to foam. The barking and growling with the three of them is loud enough that Paul is having a tough time hearing the test center. I see the owner standing by her backdoor with a smirk on her face.

"You need to call off your dogs, ma'am! He can't even hear with them going on like that!"

She just lights a cigarette and says, "Not my problem."

I look up at Paul and he is no longer trying to talk with the test center. He catches my eye, shakes his head, shifts his weight and repositions himself. The dogs go crazy when he moves.

Alright, I think. This has gone far enough. I proceed to explain that we have easement rights, meaning we are allowed access to our cable, our equipment wherever it is. It's the same for any utility.

"We've gone out of our way to work around you and now you've let

14

your dogs out. You are deliberately keeping us from being able to complete our work!"

She just stares at me. Lady, I think, you have way too much time on your hands if this is all you can think of to do this afternoon.

"Call the dogs in or I will call the police. I'm not kidding," I say. I know she won't call her dogs in. Instead, she begins screaming at Paul.

"You little pussy! Are you too scared? You fucking pussy, scared of a couple dogs!" At this outburst, it occurs to me that she may be mentally ill and/or drunk.

I walk back to the bottom of the pole and yell up, "That's it, I'm calling the cops," and walk far enough away that I can be heard when I call 911.

Paul climbs down, still being harangued by this woman, and we get in my truck and drive around the block to wait for the police. We don't wait for very long and the cops hear our side of the story before going up to her door. Paul and I wait by my truck as the two policemen talk to this woman. She is still agitated but after several minutes agrees to call off her dogs. The police stay there while Paul goes back up and within 15 minutes has completed his work.

So, two hours, two technicians, two police officers, three pit bulls and one uncooperative, possibly crazy woman later, the job was completed. Paul and I drove to a small diner for a much-deserved cup of coffee and a debriefing session.

THE WORLD IS MY URINAL

The world is my urinal. That's right. I said it. Working outside for a living means the outdoors is the office. The office has many accouterments. There are several departments. There are several types of rooms meant to accommodate a myriad of needs such as desks, work benches, tool cribs, boardrooms, break rooms and, of course, specially plumbed rooms for hers, his, and theirs.

My truck is my office, workbench, boardroom, and com center. My break room is the nearest espresso establishment, and my tool crib is back at my supervisor's office area.

The toidie? Oh, I'm sure you're certain we stop what we're doing, pack up all the tools, put away the safety gear, inform the customer we will return soon, and go find a public restroom. Riiiigghht!!

We could ask the residential customer to borrow their facilities. Now that's just rude AND gross, for them and you. I would share that these issues are not an issue at a regular business building so...

In general, where dost thou relieve thyself?

Your alley.

Behind your shed.

The far corner of your flower bed (if I'm certain you or no one else is around).

More than once, assured as to the level of privacy available while sitting on my work box, I have stood up from that position and urinated into the now empty coffee-to-go-cup.

Whewwww!!

When out on a country dirt road, that is indeed a feeling of freedom, breeze blowing through the ... well, you know what I mean, eh? At times when I have a van, that's like a personal RV. You just climb in and grab that special oversized drink cup that is a permanent part of the "tools" selection. Utility bed trucks have many swing-out bin doors that create a very nice instant outhouse. Traffic just whizzes by thinking you are digging through tools, oblivious to the obvious. Other locations, while seemingly disgusting, actually serve well. New building and housing construction often have "sump-pump" holes installed.

What? Oh, I guarantee the construction guys have made use before the porta potty was finally set up.

One favorite of mine as far as convenience goes is the floor drain in, well, just about anywhere. For instance, apartment building utility rooms, manufacturing plants, rainwater drains, and just about any place that has a grate and a pipe that goes ... away.

Once, while up a pole, on the phone, and on hold with a testing technician (you NEVER drop a call when you finally get the tester on the line) nature called on the other line. You cannot wiggle your legs while standing on pole steps very well at all. So what to do? I'm well camouflaged by the trees and that damn dog below will not shut up, so ... yep, I hike a leg up one step and give the dog something to smell.

Now, as for Number 2? Well, that's just a whole other set of stories, typically involving shovels, leaves that are not poisonous, and a level of desperation that precludes most forms of decency that would only take the subject too far south.

HOVER PEE
(OR UNISEX AND OTHER MISNOMERS)

As a woman, I would be remiss if I did not mention the dilemma of the unisex bathroom. If you're a guy reading this, you have no idea what I'm talking about, do you? No. And do you know why? It's simple: you get to pee standing up.

As I've stated, sometimes I didn't have the luxury of a choice while working as a telephone technician as to where I could use the bathroom. Sometimes I would be so relieved to not only find a bathroom I could use, but also that I got there in time, that I could almost overlook the fact that it was a unisex bathroom. Not this time.

I walked in and realized this bathroom was also being used as a stockroom and storage closet. New packs of toilet paper were stacked against the wall, right next to the cases of juice drinks and the toilet plunger. A couple of coats were hanging on nails, and a pair of boots was sitting next to the toilet.

Oh, Lord, the toilet. You know how when you're trying very hard not to look at a thing and somehow your eyes keep going back to that very thing?

Yeah, it was like that. How to describe this toilet? I'm not exaggerating when I say it had never been cleaned. In fact, I was starting to believe I may have been the first woman to enter this bathroom. Here's the thing, though: I was here, I had to go, and I had to go now. Which brings me to the art of the Hover Pee.

This is a maneuver that was necessitated by the very conditions I was presented within this grimy, dirty, cramped, smelly unisex bathroom. And let's just address this right now: it is not a unisex bathroom. Unisex is a euphemism for *It's a men's bathroom that a woman can use if she's desperate enough*. I have my jeans at my knees and I am hovering a few inches above the toilet seat, praying there's no backsplash from this distance. God knows what mutant strain of fungus is growing in that toilet bowl. I've had to do this, enough times that my thigh muscles are extraordinarily strong, like tree trunks. Because here's the other thing: this place is so filthy I don't even want to touch anything that might give me some support during the hover. I'm just Freestyle Hover Peeing.

When I'm done, I don't even wash my hands in the sink. That would mean touching the hot water handle. Nope. I'll use the cleaner I carry on my truck. At least I know where it's been. I walk outside and take a deep breath of fresh air, and I know then the unisex bathroom choice will be the last option on my list. Right after peeing in an alley.

TWO VARIATIONS OF DESPERATION

As a woman working as an outside technician, another challenge I had was finding a decent place to go to the bathroom. By a decent place, I mean somewhere that is a) preferably for women only, b) clean, and c) private. Realistically, if only one of those conditions were present I was pretty lucky.

I knew every decent convenient store location for miles around, but unfortunately, that wasn't always an option. I'll just go ahead and say it: women have to be a bit more creative when peeing in locations other than an actual bathroom. We have to be quick, too. It's not as if we can act casual in the middle of a squat - as if we're looking for something we lost while our pants are down around our ankles - like our dignity.

As I've said before, I worked in a rural area outside of the city for many years. It might be miles before I'd even see another vehicle on those country roads, and the nearest town was several minutes away. Have I mentioned that it was drilled into our heads to never, EVER ask a customer if we could use their restroom? Now, did I have to use a customer's restroom occasionally? Yes, but I bet I could count those times on one hand in my thirty years with the company. Which is why something like what I'm about to describe could happen.

I'm way out in the country, and I'm chasing down an open cable pair so I can repair it and get my customer back in service. Basically, this means that one of the two wires that it takes to bring dial tone into your house is broken, and I have to find where to splice it back together.

I've been working on this for about an hour, and I have to pee. There's no way I'm driving all the way back into town to go to the bathroom at our central office. At this point, I'm fairly certain I wouldn't make it back in time anyway. I'm just going to pull over to the side of the road, open my driver's door and pee very quickly next to my truck.

I don't hear any vehicles, and there are no houses in sight. I drop my jeans and am mid-stream when I hear and feel something rumbling on the road up ahead. I'm on the other side of a rise in the road, and the rumbling is getting louder but I can't see anything coming. Frantically I am trying to finish and pull up my jeans at the same time as I see a school bus coming over the top of the hill. Really? A school bus? It had to be an entire bus full of children that saw me, not some half blind farmer on a tractor?

By the time the school bus passes me, I am standing up, holding my jeans up with one hand and waving at them with the other, praying I got my pants up before any of the kids or the driver saw me. All day I waited for a page from my supervisor telling me I was seen and that the sight of my white ass has traumatized several nine-year-old children. Fortunately, that page didn't come, but I did learn a valuable lesson that day.

Next time, find a tree.

I had a new technician shadowing me, a guy who had been working in the business office. Interestingly enough, men would hire on at Ma Bell in 'non-traditional male' job positions (service representatives, operators, etc.) hoping to transfer outside at some point. This tech had just finished pole climbing school and installation school so he had some basic knowledge, but like any job, you learn more from observing and working hands-on.

David and I are at this customer's house to install a second landline for their teenage daughter's birthday present. A private line for teenagers was a great gift (for the kid and the parents), and we often would be asked to come during school hours so as to keep it a surprise. I've actually lied a couple of times to kids who have come home while their 'surprise' line was being installed, saying I was there to repair the main line.

So, we are working with a small window of opportunity, as we have about two hours before this young lady will be home from school. David knows this, and I am explaining what I'm doing and why as I work. I have him pay out the new aerial service wire between the house and the pole as I carry my 28-foot extension ladder to the backyard. He's asking me questions and watching as I set up my ladder. He is supposed to attach the wire to the house as I do the work on the pole.

I clip the aerial service wire to my belt and ascend the ladder, belt off and open up the terminal. Well, shoot, my dial tone isn't where it's supposed to be. It takes a few minutes to figure out two cable pairs are transposed, and then I find my number. I look back and see David carrying the 6-foot stepladder to the house, and I yell at him, "Go ahead and attach it at the house. I've got it attached up here," and he yells back, "OK."

A few minutes go by. I'm about to finish and I realize the line is still lying on the ground. I look around from my vantage point of 25 feet in the air. The stepladder is set up at the house but no sign of David. I look over to my truck parked on the side street; he isn't there either. What the hell?

I start looking everywhere, doing a 360-degree scan from the pole, and that's when I see him in our customer's flower garden on the opposite side of the backyard. He is urinating in her garden. In broad daylight. His back is to the customer's house, but he could clearly be seen by two different neighbors, should they be looking out their backdoors. I am so stunned I can't even say anything for a few seconds. Then I find my voice.

"Are you kidding me, David?" I yell at him. He holds his free hand up as if to say, "hold on," and then he is zipping up his pants. I have unbelted and begin descending the ladder while trying to remain calm. He is starting to climb up the stepladder, and I tell him to come

24

with me to the truck. He follows me and tells me he's sorry, but he really had to go to the bathroom and couldn't hold it anymore.

"David, don't you ever, EVER do that again. I hope no one calls in about this because I'm not about to explain this to our supervisor."

"I knew we didn't have much time and I didn't want to slow us down," he explains.

"You could have taken my truck to the closest convenience store or said something before we got here. I know you think you were being discreet, but you could've been seen. Don't torpedo your technician job before you even get started!" I can see that he is embarrassed, and I lower my voice.

"Look, there isn't a tech that hasn't peed outside or somewhere that isn't an actual bathroom, including me, okay? It's one of the challenges of this job. But you have got to plan and think about this ahead of time and choose the location more wisely."

"I will. I promise. And I'm sorry. I really am."

I know he is, and I say so. I tell him I will install the jack while he hooks the service wire up to the interface. As I go inside the house I brace myself in case our customer has seen David peeing on her mums, but she doesn't say anything. I tell her we're almost finished, and she is happy and excited that we got everything done in time. She tells me she will wrap up the pink Princess phone (remember those?) and give it to her daughter on her birthday, which is two days from now.

I smile and tell her I'm glad we could help make that happen, thank the lady, and head back outside. David is at the truck, has everything put up, and is waiting for me. I tell him our customer said nothing about him, and he looks quite relieved.

"Ok then," he says, "where's our next job? What are we doing there?" He really is so excited to be working outside.

I smile at him and tell him we have one stop to make before the next job ... the convenience store.

EEWWW!

I know you are already cringing because you feel it coming. That's right, gross stories. Some buildings, some residences, some people, some animals are just ... eewww!

My town is one of those industrial cities that, back in the 1940s, erected temporary neighborhoods for the war-time build-up. One major problem with such a project is that the concept is inherently flawed. When people move into a temporary housing development, they stay. For years. For decades. Their grandchildren live there 40 years after Ma and Pa factory workers kick the rivet bucket and go to the Union Hall meeting in the sky.

So presently, grandson factory worker is living in a house that was paid for 10 years after the first move in. The government is too embarrassed to attempt to reclaim said temporary property, as well as the fact that the good old county is collecting property tax revenue on land the federal government developed to begin with.

Next part in the equation is the current resident has not done any kind of repairs or improvements since grandpa installed that brand-spankin' new swamp-cooler in the living-room window in 1961.

"What the hell, it still works all right. Besides, we always go to the lake in the RV during the summer weekends," I've heard stated.

An interesting fact about temp housing neighborhoods back in the war-era is they were not subject to the same public utility codes as today. Hell, they weren't always subject to the in-place codes back then.

For instance, the width, height, and depths of easements for electric, phone lines, city water lines, and ... sewer lines.

Over the course of twenty, thirty, seventy years down the road, the weather has a tendency to wash away the soil off a property that, well, has no grass anyway. Kind of hard to grow foliage on a dirt lot that has had some kind of dead motor vehicle (or four) parked on it for 50 years.

So, rain has washed off six, no, ten inches of no-grow soil over the years and exposed, what was only buried eight inches to begin with, instead of the current code of six feet... the house sewer line.

I will bet you can imagine why the city and county bury sewer lines six feet down.

Yes, for the same reason they will bury you six feet down. It smells. Bad.

Ok, here is my scenario:

It is the dead of winter. For being cold, it is a beautifully sunny, yet snow-covered day.

I don't mind cold when it is dry outside. The crisp but sunny view is pleasant. I'm only slightly annoyed that I have to traverse the crawl space of this "vintage tiny-house." These temp homes are essentially built-on-site mobile homes. They are propped up on foundations no more stable than the cinder blocks and glorified car jacks trailer homes are placed upon.

You now understand I am crawling under something that could

collapse and kill me. (You're with me, right?) Here I go, on hands and knees, wishing the cold air could suppress the festering, fifty-year-old perfume of three generations of factory workers lodged into this small airspace. I've got a hold of the new premise wire I fed through from the hole I just drilled down from the kitchen. Pulling the wire along, I back out of the large crawl space opening that has not been covered since 1978, connect the wire to network interface, and I should now have dial-tone to the new phone jack inside.

As I'm gathering my tools into my work box, which is right next to the crawl space access hole, I can hear the distinct echo of plumbing flush under the house as well as right behind me (behind me???).

I turn to look across the blanket of winter white and just a few feet away, in a snow-melted-away hole, I see a puff of steam emanating from an exposed sewer line that had the top side broken and caved in for however many years.

I glanced just in time to view the Good Ship Brownie-Plop and accompanying confetti stream by.

Go ahead and say it, "Eewww!"

AS SEEN FROM SPACE

Working aloft. That is the usual technical term for being "up a pole." Aerial, in the air, wood monkey, gaffer, lineman (bad Glen Campbell jokes to be ignored).

All these and other terms are used to describe access to a perspective on the world most of you will never have. That is, eighteen to thirty feet above your house. Beauty, intrigue, inspiration, horror, disgust, and yes, blatant blandness. We've seen them all.

High above the utility easement, staring into the neighbor's backyard can reveal quite a bit.

You've been jealous of the neighbor's in-ground pool. Don't bother; it has not been cleaned since they installed it 4 years ago. By the way, are you missing a cat?

Oh ... you meant the other neighbor, the one the sultry noises always come from. Well, let me just say the view is, "Hello, Mrs. Robinson!"

Hoarding of various items easily occurs behind high fences. I find it interesting that some types of objects seem to captivate our attention span so much that we think we must fill the entire universe with said objects.

Dead automobiles must be grouped to resemble the castle that one's ancestors lost in battle to some Viking army. Bicycles, arranged properly, could indeed serve to be the fake wrought-iron fence you dearly want but will never actually purchase. Dogs (yes, primates hoard canines) often become evidence of some psychotic homo-sapiens inner desire to be Mother Superior to a sort of orphanage of four-legged "Lost Boys." Gardens. Well, let's just say that while being a gentleman farmer seems noble and all, unless you actually make it a full-time daily gig, that hobby will run amuck to the point that the zucchini will overtake the deck.

There are indeed many other forms of nature to enjoy while aloft. Simply staring off into the urban or suburban forest is delightful. Looking up at trees from the ground is ok but gazing into the tree as if in a tree house is often gorgeous. In spring, your head is among the budding leaves and flowering brush while the birds return and start the neighborhood chatter.

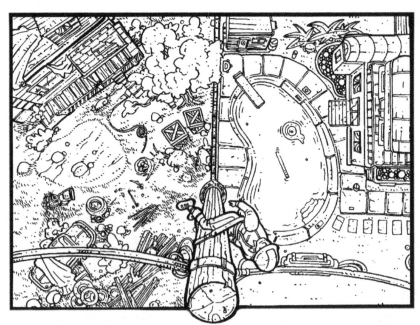

Summertime envelops one in the lush green while shading you from the midday heat. Being eye level with the telephone cable, you stare down the length as if looking out at a lone highway that disappears into the horizon.

Fall brings the crisp air as well as the art exhibit of color and random pre-winter nesting of squirrels and other resident wild animals.

Winter runs the extremes. Being aloft in the sub-freezing wind, rain, snow, and sleet is by no means a picnic. Yet, when the storms calm and the sun peeks out to reveal the ice-covered, bare tree branches as well as the equally adorned utilities, the image is that of a surreal fairy-tale movie.

As the street vernacular goes, "Best day at work, ever."

BACK ALLEY ENCOUNTERS

A beautiful morning in the back alleys presented yet another unexpected introduction and opportunity.

This particular repair order places me in an older, residential, city alleyway. My truck is parked in the alley just a few yards in front of the pole I've ascended. I'm now belted on at the terminal height and working on a broken drop wire. Everything is going status quo ... till now.

Here comes a car, down the one-lane alley.

Have I mentioned what an annoying pain in the ass these situations are? A huge utility vehicle with flashing yellow lights and orange cones circling the vehicle and J.Q. Public can't figure out that the alley is blocked.

Oh yeah, you've guessed it. These types of folks pull right up and sit there in the car waiting for you to move. Sometimes they even have the audacity to insist we move *now.*

In the past, I have indeed climbed back down the pole, bitching under my breath, moved the cones, pulled on through the alley so as to accommodate the public's urgent need to pull into, no, seriously ... what?

Yes, some SOBs just drive through the alley and drive off down the street. They did not need me to move. They were just too lazy and or stupid to back out of the situation they created for themselves.

Yeah, it's happened and will again.

Yet, my jaded, cynical disdain for most of humanity is about to get pleasantly and surprisingly fucked with.

The aforementioned car pulls right up behind me, the engine is turned off, and a rather well-built blonde steps out and heads toward the backyard drive of the adjacent house.

"Ma'am, I apologize for being in the way. I'll be done in just a few minutes, so you can get to your drive," I inform her.

"No problem. I'm running in and right back out. There's room for me to turn around," she replies in a friendly tone.

Cluster-you-know-what averted, I continue my aerial repair work.

In just a couple of minutes, the nice lady comes back out. She stops and stands some 20 feet from the pole area to watch me work. I'm thinking, "Now what?"

"Hey."

"Yes, ma'am?"

"You married?"

"Uh ..." (Brain, stop stuttering) "... well, uh, yes, ma'am."

"Humph ... you want my number anyway?" she gleefully offers.

Okay, brain, which version of stupid are we going with today? Hmm ... the high road of dumb. Good plan.

"I AM flattered, ma'am. I'd best decline. But ... thanks!"

"Well, okay. Have a good day."

She takes all that exuberance, shoves it back into the car, and drives away.

I spend a few moments collecting my delightfully shaken ego and finish the wire work. Back down the pole, I test the line at the house. All okay. I put away the tools, orange cones, inspect around the truck, grab a drink of water, and jump back into the cab of the truck.

As I start to buckle up, there's a piece of paper in the way. What's this say?

"I'll be damned ... 'Jenny, 555-867-5309'."

So many dilemmas.

BACK ALLEY ENCOUNTERS PART TWO

The Dark Force.

Ticket #123xyz,

Name: J. Q. Public

Service Address: 1527 S. Some Place

Note: Apartment-garage upstairs.

Yep ... there it is.

Okay, around to the alley to get to the terminal pole.

Trouble report: No dial tone, Test: Open out.

Terminal: (Rear of) 1530 Other-side Dr.

No ... keep driving ... yeah, here we are.

There's the terminal. There's the customer's apartment.

Gather paperwork info. Now to get tools and body-belt to go up pole.

Open truck door ... wha-th ... what now?

Great, another moron that thinks the alleyway is their personal driveway.

Geez buddy, you're awfully close. Hey ... now there's a car pulling up behind him.

What the ... now there's one in *front* of me?

Whoa ... those look like unmarked police department detective cars.

I'm now watching this group of three suit-wearing detective types leap out of the cars, pistols drawn, march double-time past my truck.

As they pass by my door the last one says to me, "Stay in the truck!"

"Yes, SIR!" I say to myself.

These guys run up to the door of *my* customer's address and bang on his door; he opens it, and they march inside. In about one minute, the occupant comes out in cuffs. They march him down the stairs, past my truck, toss him into one of the nondescript sedans, and all three cars roar back out the alley.

Now what?

I'm here to repair the service. The customer is now ... well, *gone* and not likely to be back anytime soon, most likely going to be disconnected for non-pay. Already spent too much time on the ticket to call it a "No Access."

I fill out the paperwork; "Drop Repaired, ticket complete."

Lunchtime.

CHEATING DEATH

Electricity was a part of that most often. Or climbing a pole, driving, and various species of animals.

I was installing several lines in a new convenience store. Contractors everywhere, it's all coming together and starts looking more like a convenience store and less like the after-the-tornado picture. I was bringing in two underground service wires, so I had to drill a hole through cinder block, which meant using my hammer drill and the biggest masonry bit I had. I brought the drill, the bit, and an extension cord in and hooked everything up. I decided to drill about six inches to one side of where the main electrical line came in underneath the junction box. So, I started drilling, and it's taking me pushing with my knee against the handle of the drill to get through the cinderblock. And ok, it wasn't the sharpest bit, but I felt it give as it went through to the outside.

The instant the drill bit went through, the lights in the entire place flickered for about two seconds and then came back on and stayed on. I got a sick feeling in my stomach and pulled my drill bit out of the wall. What used to be an eighteen-inch drill bit was now about five inches long. There was an electrician standing on a six-foot ladder working up in the ceiling a couple feet away, and he looked at me and said, "I bet you're glad that hammer drill is grounded right about now, aren't you?"

Yes, I was. The main electric lines were in a conduit that was offset from the main junction box, not in the middle as it usually was. I managed to drill right through the center of it. If I'd tried to measure it and purposefully do that, I would miss.

I called my supervisor and he called KG&E and let them know what happened - they would have to replace the entire underground electric cables back to the terminal at the rear of the property. So, I knew this would be a good time to leave! No way was I going to tell a single contractor - besides, the electrician already knew so it would get around pretty quickly - and I did not want to be there when KG&E showed up. It was embarrassing and costly, albeit completely unintentional. I gathered my drill and electrical cord, what was left of my drill bit and my tools, and I got the hell out of there.

I think it was a toss-up which bothered me more--almost being electrocuted or the embarrassment.

This next story supports my assertion that just because you think you can pull it off doesn't mean it's necessarily a good idea to try it.

This occurred while I was working on the payphone crew. That's all we did was install and repair pay phones. Remember those? The first choice of communication for drug dealers everywhere.

I'm in an old building that my customer is converting into a laundromat, and they want a pay phone installed in the lobby so people won't be asking to use their business lines.

I am using the customer's giant twelve-foot stepladder to climb up and look in the ceiling to see if there are any existing phone lines I might be able to use. No such luck.

40

Now, I know I should run a new line from the front of the building to the back. It's a long, narrow building, approximately 400-feet, which means if I run it inside through the ceiling it will involve moving that stepladder every few feet while pulling the wire the entire length of the building.

Or I could climb up on the roof and see if there is a way to run it across, may be attached to a conduit. I get my 28-foot ladder out and extend it two rungs above the roofline and climb up.

Once I get up there I see that what looks like the roof line is a four-foot high wall, so I must swing my leg over and drop down onto the roof. That was fine; I had no problem with that. It was after I scoped out the roof and decided I could run a wire up there that I went back to my ladder and realized there was no way in hell I'd be able to get up on that wall and step onto my extension ladder. Not safely, anyway, and I had serious doubts I could pull it off even if I managed to get up on the wall. I do NOT want to have to call one of my buddies on the crew or my supervisor. There's got to be a way to get off this roof.

And then I saw it: a way down. The building was L-shaped and there was another business next door. Next to it was a storage shed, and I believed I could jump from the roof onto the shed roof, then drop down from there to the ground.

I convinced myself it could be done. So, imagine the shock and horror I experienced when - still airborne between the building and the roof of the shed - I realized not only had I misjudged the distance of the drop to the shed roof, I had also seriously miscalculated how steep the shed roof was. When I say miscalculated I really mean I didn't even think about it.

My feet hit the roof, I threw myself down on my belly, and I am sliding downwards. With my left hand, I am clawing for something solid along the roofline when my fingers are slashed open by the edge of the flashing.

Of course, I let go at that moment. I become aware of yet another misjudgment on my part which is the distance from the shed roof to the ground.

I land on my feet for about a half second and am propelled backward where I land on my ass. I'm kind of sitting there, letting my brain catch up to what my body just went through when I look down at my left hand and realize how badly I'm bleeding. I hold my hand out, palm up, and I can see the tendon in my finger. That's how deep the cut was.

I close my eyes thinking, "Okay, do not look at that again."

So, of course, I had to call my supervisor and let him know I was on my way to the hospital. At that time, we had mobile phones in our vehicles, so I called him and left a message then called our dispatch center and told them what was happening, asking if they could continue to try and reach my boss.

Someone would have to come out and get my extension ladder.

I wrapped my hand in paper towels and drove myself to the ER. My supervisor showed up with one of my co-workers, which was a good thing because I'd been given some pain meds after they stitched me up. Twelve stitches in my middle finger and seven in my ring finger. Oh, and a slight sprain in my right ankle.

My boss would drive me home and my co-worker would drive my truck.

Someone else on my crew got my ladder.

I did take a lot of kidding about this incident, and deservedly so, but it could've been a whole lot worse as far as injuries go so I'm grateful for that. Never got up on a roof like that again.

HAIL NO

It was a typical spring day. Slightly overcast with a touch of moisture in the air. Just right to feel comfortable in the middle of the day.

I'm at the backside of a tiny tract house, occupied by a sweet, three-generation family of Southeast Asian (very recent) immigrants. I'm beginning the initial testing at the interface on some simple, unmemorable trouble report.

The sky has rapidly darkened, and I start to feel a little extra wind and a considerable amount of air dampness. Soon this turns to a few scattered droplets.

A few more moments go by, and light amounts of pea-size hail begin to drop. No big deal, however, my hard hat is in the truck stow bin in the back-pick-up bed with my climbing gear, so I take this as an excuse to just go back to the truck, finish my coffee and read the paper while this bit of weather blows through.

I get comfy in the cab of the pick-up truck. This is a regular cab truck with the utility bed on the back. As I have a sip, the hail continues, then becomes quarter size. Boy, I'm glad I stopped when I did. That might smart if I had gotten smacked in the noggin.

I turn on the radio and hear weather reports immediately. The commentator advises that "Tornadoes are often preceded by hail directly to the left." Well, that's good. That means a potential tornado will miss me by a few miles, I smirk to myself.

My smirk was followed by a loud smack on the hood of the truck by of a chunk of hail the size of a lemon. HOLY SHIT! just replaced my smirk. A few dozen more of these lemons cascade. Geez. Now the deafening hammer-strikes overtake all sound. Orange size hail in the billions (no exaggeration) is coming down all around my truck and the neighborhood as far as I can see, which by now is not far at all.

The windshield of the truck has, this moment, been shattered. I have just covered it from the inside with the cardboard sunshade and my briefcase to shore up support. What the hell do I think I'm doing? This isn't going to protect anything. I gotta get into that house!

Remember my damn hard hat is in the back?
Well, I grab my straw hat and cover it with the cardboard sunshade, throw open the truck door and haul ass up to the porch. I knock furiously, yell, "HELP!" more furiously, and, in seconds, the father of the house lets me in and slams the door.

Hail chucks are smashing through the windows of this house and shooting across the floor into adjacent rooms. The mother and children are scared to death and begin to cry. I help gather the family into the core hallway, tell mom and dad to grab blankets and pillows for shield padding. Then they direct my attention to the bedridden grandmother in the back bedroom. Just as we begin to roll her bed into the hallway, about 5 solid minutes of a scene from "Apocalypse Now" comes to a complete halt.

Dead silence.

The manic fear-driven scene has ended.

The father and I step outside to a bizarre, surreal scene. The streets in all directions are over-the-curb-full of massive baseball-size hailstones. The wind has stopped as well. In all directions, there is a two-foot-deep blanket of fog from the ice-laden street and yards on this, once again, mild spring day.

Well, just another day at the telco. We run through a war zone and then step into a B-rated horror film.

THE FIRES OF ST. ELMO

Most likely, few of you have any idea what in the world St. Elmo's fire is. That is the point; it is not of the world. St Elmo's fire is the child born from the love affair between lighting and earthbound object

It is a magical thing of beauty. A beauty random and completely unpredictable. Even lightning itself is easier to catch.

You can schedule a trip to see the Aurora Borealis. Choosing to see St. Elmo's fire is not an option. It chooses you. When it does choose you, be quick. I don't mean be quick to see. I mean be quick not to die.

Lightning can and will hit anything, not just something high in the air like a tree, tall building or a power pole. I personally know a guy who has been hit by lightning three separate times. Yes, he's still alive, walking, talking and in possession of at least most of his marbles. We joke his tombstone will read, "Die Already."

I segue for a brief science lesson: Lightning happens when the negative charges (electrons) in the bottom of the cloud are attracted to the positive charges (protons) in the ground.

The accumulation of electric charges has to be great enough to overcome the insulating properties of air. When this happens, a stream of negative charges pours down towards a high point where positive charges have clustered due to the pull of the thunderhead. The connection is made, and the protons rush up to meet the electrons and the other-worldly Tango begins.

At this point, we see lightning and hear thunder. A bolt of lightning heats the air along its path causing it to expand rapidly. Thunder is the sound caused by rapidly expanding air, just like when you clap your hands, you create a tiny, little sonic BOOM!

OK, even if all that explanation did not sink in, you certainly know enough to get out of the way of lightning.

Me, too.

It's another "up the pole" day. I'm belted on comfortably; no trees encroaching on me and the terminal. Cables and drops are tidy enough to be easy to work on and around. It is heavy overcast, cloudy, cool and somewhat serene that afternoon.

(Note: We techs avoid the rainy situations. It's damn uncomfortable, messy and, well, a power surge from a power pole transformer, let alone lightning, can fry your ass in a New York second.)

I'm not worried. There's no storm ... yet.

I'm working away repairing a pair in this cable terminal. I start to hear a little rumble off in the distance. Well, the clouds are finally forming some trouble. I don't see or smell any moisture, but I speed up a little to avoid getting wet.

In another minute or two, I hear a heavy, rolling roar building; then, from what seems like only a block or so away, I hear a large roar and then a sharp, loud, "CRACK."

Now, I recognize that tune.

I let go of the steel cable strand and lean my upper body back as far as possible to avoid touching anything made of metal.

Then I watch ... bzz-vvvoooossshhhh ... crackles ... bzzz ...

A faded pale blue, one foot in diameter, egg shape ball of St. Elmo's Fire zips past on the cable strand, two feet from my face as fast as ... well, lightning.

When you see something mystical and damned scary for the first time, a little mental shock is expected.

I likely had my mouth clenched tightly while simultaneously muttering, "f-fuuuuuuu ... CK!"

I began to undo my safety belt strap, avoiding contact with anything metal.

You know how it is when you get a little static zap of the carpet?

Yeah, well, the residual voltage from that lightning zap would be similar-to-being smacked with a sledge-hammer.

I make my way down touching only the wood part of the pole (thank goodness it was dry). Still, in a bit of shock, I make it to the ground.

Uh ... coffee time, I'm thinking.

I'll finish that job later.

It is rare that we actually see the bizarre damage brought by lightning and the ensuing St. Elmo carnage as it happens. Typically, we see every day, the collateral damage.

Hell, we make entire careers out of repairing said damage.

HOW COLD IS IT?

It's Christmas Eve around 3 o'clock in the afternoon, and it is freaking cold out. The temperature is 10 degrees, and the wind is blowing 20 mph, so the wind chill is about 10 below.

This is one of Ma Bell's busiest times because we discount the price on additional lines, and it's a great gift for teenagers. These orders are usually during school hours because, of course, it's supposed to be a surprise. Also, the jack needs to NOT SHOW - she can't see it before Christmas morning! I had to lie to one kid who came home before I was done; I told him I was working on the main line. Now THAT is Customer Service!

So, while most Ma Bell employees who work in an office building are having Christmas parties, we installers are out completing the day's service orders. No resentment here. Just saying when we call in because we need support, please turn down the music and put down the vodka and tonic you think you're hiding from everyone and DO YOUR JOB for three minutes. Jeez. But I digress...

I'm installing my last additional line for the day. My customer can't believe I'm out working in this cold, and she has offered me coffee (which I will take her up on once I get down from here). "Here" is on my extension ladder about 18 feet in the air, suspended on the cable strand between two poles. In this wind, everything moves as the gusts intensify--the strand, the ladder, and me. I am belted around the ladder, and the strand and I trust my equipment, but still ... this is Mother Nature and she ALWAYS wins. I have a healthy respect for her power.

My fingers are numb, my nose is running, and through three layers of clothes, I can still feel the wind cutting through. Then I realize my eyes are watering and freezing on my eyelashes. Literally, I have frozen drops on my eyelashes. I have one thought: they aren't paying me enough money to work out in this shit.

I finished the job, my customer was happy, and I left with a cup of good, strong coffee. Ever since then, my bar for being cold has been that afternoon. If my eyelashes aren't frozen, then I've been colder.

HELL HATH NO FURY

I worked out in little farming towns outside of the city for many years. I enjoyed the change from working in the city, and there were different challenges when working in the outlying areas.

One major difference was that the central offices were unmanned, meaning no one was there on a permanent basis. The central office, simply speaking, is where the dial tone comes from. There are certain steps that have to occur for the dial tone to leave the central office on the assigned cable pair going out to the field, and in these unmanned offices, it was often up to the outside technician to do this.

An actual frame attendant would be there in the morning for a short amount of time to do the work for whatever orders were due that day, but if anything changed or went wrong, it fell to the technician to make the changes in the office.

This was the case on the service order I was working on. The cable pair was open, it wasn't getting to the terminal I needed it to get to, and I had to find a good cable pair. Ideally, we could pull up a record of what was available to us and test it with a frame attendant. In a manned central office, this might take ten minutes if all goes well.

The town I was working in had an unmanned office, so I was testing the available cable pairs trying to find one that looked like it went all the way back to the office from my customer's location.

Did I mention that I was about twelve miles away from the office?

So, I call the office on the off-chance that another tech has stopped in and may answer the phone, saving me a whole lot of time and travel. There are only two lines to call into this small office, and when I dial the main number, it's busy.

"OK," I'm thinking, "This is good because that means someone is in the office and can help me."

I wait a couple of minutes and call again, but I get the busy signal again. I decided to call on the other number, hoping they'll pick up.

It's a professional courtesy, in my opinion, to help another co-worker out in this situation.

Well, the other number rings. And rings and rings. I hang up and immediately call the main line again. Still busy. I feel the first stirrings of anger and disbelief that someone is in the central office and refuses to answer an incoming call.

I wait a couple more minutes, call the main line and it's busy. The second line continues to ring endlessly. I call the main line one more time, and when it's busy, I throw my headset down on the ground and shout a few choice words up to the sky. I hook up a tone signal on the cable pair I think I can use (if I get the tone in the central office, then I know there is continuity all the way and it's a good pair), let my customer know what I'm doing, and jump in my truck to drive into town.

All the way in I am thinking about who it is in the office who won't answer the phone. If it's anyone other than a tech or a frame attendant, I could cut them some slack, maybe, but if it's a technician I'm not sure what I'll do.

I pull into the parking lot behind the building, and there's a cable repairman's truck parked there; I know immediately who it is.

I punch in the code to get in the back door and as I walk into the mainframe room, there at the desk sits Bob, the cable repairman. He has his boots off, his feet up on the desk, a newspaper in his hands and the phone cradled under his ear. He's still talking, and I don't know if he's heard me come in. But he's about to.

I am striding towards the desk and I raise my voice and say, "Would it fucking kill you to get off your ass and answer the other line when you're in here?" He jumps at the sound of my voice, tells whoever is on the other end he'll call them back, and has the nerve to say to me, "Were you calling in? I didn't hear it."

"BULLSHIT YOU DIDN'T HEAR IT! Are you kidding me? I called in half a dozen times on the second line and you just kept ignoring it, and now I've driven in from about fifteen miles out to take care of this when you could have handled it in about three minutes if you'd had the courtesy to get off your ass!"

His mouth is hanging open, and when I finish, he asks if there's anything he can do to help me now. Really?

At this point in my career, I had as much if not more seniority than most of the guys I worked with. I'd been with the company right around 23 years at the time of this incident, and, as you may have deduced by now, I didn't have a lot of patience for laziness or incompetence. Nor was I shy about expressing my dissatisfaction.

I was at the mainframe and had found my cable pair with the tone on it, so I knew I could use it. I was in the process of making the change to the new cable pair when I started talking to Bob again. He is still sitting at the desk in his fucking stocking feet.

"No, no thanks, Bob. Don't get up. God forbid. Call your friend back. I'll be out of here in a minute. Sorry for interrupting you."

I finish up and walk past Bob on my way to the women's bathroom before I head back out to my customer. He won't make eye contact with me and folds his newspaper and straightens the desk up. I look over to my right into the room next door, a huge space where some new equipment is to be installed, and that's when I see it.

Bob has a putting green set up in the room. There are a couple of putters, several golf balls, the green, and the cup. I can't even say I'm surprised. Hell, why wouldn't he have a putting green in the central office? Why wouldn't he practice his putting while he's ignoring the phone? I ducked my head back in the room on the way out just to see if there was a wet bar at the other end.

I had just received word that my transfer had come through, and I was due to report up there in a few weeks. I was going to give Bob a little surprise right before I left.

I bided my time and hatched my plan. I told two of my trusted buddies what I was going to do, mostly so I could hear about any fallout after I was gone.

Two days before I was due to leave I drove up to the central office in that little town. No one was there except me and my bottle of Gorilla Glue. I lined up all ten of Bob's golf balls in a perfect row and glued every one of them to the putting green. I cannot overstress the amount of satisfaction this gave me. I did talk to my buddies the next week and they reported the putting green had been removed. Bob never said a word to anyone.

I'VE GOT A POLE YOU CAN CLIMB

In our city are several aircraft plants; some of the biggest employers in this city and when they are operating at full capacity, there are three shifts, so they are running 24 hours a day. This makes for some interesting dynamics, like strip clubs being full at 8 a.m., and customers drinking around the same time at their homes. No big deal, just having some drinks after work, right?

I arrive at my customer's house around 8:30 a.m., and as soon as he opens the door, I know he's been drinking by the smell and the way he looks me up and down before saying, "You sure you can do this job?"

I have grown used to this, being one of the first women to work as an outside technician. So, I just smile, assure him I'm up to it, and we go inside so he can show me where this second line is going to be installed. As I'm going back to my truck I hear him talking to someone in the house, saying something about lawn chairs.

Coming around the corner of his house into the backyard, where I will be running a new overhead line in from the pole to the house, I see my customer and his friend sitting in two lawn chairs with a cooler of beer between them, strategically placed so they can watch me as I work. I've become used to this as well; people are curious, I get that. Women haven't been doing this kind of work for all that long and it's not unusual for someone to watch me work. I guess seeing is believing.

So, I pay out the overhead line, attach it to my climbing belt and climb up the pole. I'm done up there in a few minutes, climb down and set up my six-foot step ladder, so I can attach the line to the house. I'm up on the ladder, just finished attaching the line when I hear my customer say, "I've got a pole you can climb."

I stop what I'm doing, step off the ladder, and turn around. I look from my customer to his buddy, who is clearly embarrassed and is shaking his head slowly, no more amused than I am. My customer is leering at me with an expression on his face somewhere between a smirk and an I-like-child-pornography kind of grin.

I walk right up to him and, in an even tone I say, "You need to keep your mouth shut the rest of the time I'm here. If I hear one more word from you I will tear down everything I've done, and you can wait another two weeks for us to send a man out here to do this. Do you understand what I'm saying?"

My customer's jaw had gone slack, but he nods. His friend is smiling at me, and I get the feeling he appreciates my directness. I also get the feeling his buddy has probably embarrassed himself before on more than one occasion.

The two men go inside the house, and I call my supervisor from the interface, letting him know what happened in case he gets a phone call from my customer. I finished the job without any further comments from my customer.

As a matter of fact, there were several occasions when I called my various supervisors to apprise them of certain situations and my responses to said situations.

THE MASKED MAULER

Part of being on someone's property to install or repair their phone service often involved dealing with the customer's pets. Domestic and exotic, cute and cuddly or downright dangerous and scary.

One of my most memorable moments came when I arrived at this customer's house to repair their line.

It was a small house up north of the city, with evidence of small children scattered about in the form of toys and clothes and bikes with training wheels. As I walked through the living room to the kitchen where the wall phone was located, my customer asked me if I was okay with animals.

"You mean a dog? Sure, I have a dog myself, so no problem," I answered.

"Well, we don't have a dog, but let me introduce you to Sid," my customer said with a smile. She disappeared into a back bedroom, and I'm thinking it must be a cat she's talking about. I take the phone off the wall and am starting to test it when I hear her say, "Here he is!" I turn around to see my customer holding a leash which goes around the corner into the hall. Does she have her cat on a leash?

Unusual but not unheard of.

"Come on, Sid. Don't be shy! Come meet the phone lady," she coaxes the as-yet-unseen Sid.

I hear a scuffling, scratching sound, and around the corner comes the biggest raccoon I've ever seen. Or maybe it was just being a mere six feet from it that made it seem bigger. Sid was clearly not hurting for food, but it wasn't just the size of him that got my attention as much as his feet. On the end of these front feet were razor sharp claws. I'm talking Edward-freaking-Scissorhands. Now Sid is standing on his back legs, and I am backing up without even knowing it.

"It's okay!" my customer is trying to reassure me. "I can let him off his leash and he won't hurt you. He usually roams around the house when he isn't up in the tree in the backyard."

Let him off his leash? Oh, hell no. Then I catch a glimpse of Sid's front teeth, and I am more certain than ever if it came to a battle between Sid and his claws and teeth versus me with my screwdriver in my hand, I am well and truly screwed.

"No, no, no ... do NOT take that leash off! I'm not kidding! I will leave!" I say as I estimate the distance between me and the back door.

"He's harmless," she insists, "I let him out around my kids!"

Okay, now I also have to call Child Protective Services.

"Please put him either outside or back where he was before."

She finally sees that I am serious. She kind of shakes her head, as if it's difficult to understand why a person might be uncomfortable being in a kitchen with an omnivore who weighs fifty pounds and has the ability to rip me to shreds in a few seconds.

"Ok, I'll take him outside then." I back away from the door, keeping my eyes on Sid while she leads him out. He waddles over to the door and, just as he's stepping over the threshold, he looks back at me and our eyes meet.

I'm pretty sure he's thinking "I will cut you, bitch."

DOGS I HAVE KNOWN

While there are many types of animals, the dominant flavor of pet we technicians encounter barks and bites. Most are friends; some others are diabolical enemies. Well actually, WE are the enemy. You see, we are complete strangers invading their territory.

The pets' attitudes range from paranoid fear to ecstatic glee at our arrival. Not only do we look different, we smell different. Sometimes worse than different; we may smell like another dog.

While it was enjoyable during the previous customer premise visit to pet and pat little Fluffy the Bichon Frise, the next ticket location provides another new acquaintance, Rex the German-Pit-Rot-Box-Pincher mutant at the machine shop. He thinks I smell like a Fluffy snack. Rex is likely to eat me, fuck me, or piss on me.

This paradox serves to set the tone for this next story which I call ...

THE IRISH SETTER WITH NEW PUPPIES.

Hell, that's all I need to say, is it not?

You already know the picture. A typically regal animal: loving, vibrant, eager to fetch anything at all as long as you can keep throwing. Most of the time I have been greeted with a wag, a stick, muddy paws, or simple complacency.

Not today.

I have been dispatched to another side of a neighborhood where slovenly is next to satanic.

It's not that the residents don't take care of their property; it's just that, it's not their property, so ... who gives a shit?

So, what we have are cars parked on the front lawn, lawn chairs and BBQ smokers in the driveway, all the guys leaning into the bed of a pickup truck of questionable functionality and the obligatory ... WHO'S-GOT-THE-MOST-BADASS-PIT-ON-THE-BLOCK?

(Did I get all the socio-stereo-types in there? Yeah, they are all the same, *no matter* whose 'hood you're in. *Ah gar-on-tee.*)

Anyway, I walk around to the backyard. Easy enough, no fences. In older made-to-rent-house neighborhoods, the landlords rarely ponied up for fences.

So, as I cruise around to the back, the first thing I notice is the now pissed off Irish Setter Mama. She has her new pups nearby, and she is on a rather healthy, albeit short, dog chain connected to her dog house.

I watch this raging mother for a couple of moments to see how close she is to my interface box on the house as well as whether she is going to break free.

Well, the distance is a comfortable one, and she seems secured. Mad as hell but secured. She is barking like crazy and foaming at the mouth.

The customer is standing nearby, watching my work tasks and blithely ignoring the noisy Setter. I discover I need to replace the drop wire entirely, so I drag a new wire up the aerial pole and make the terminal connection first.

I then proceed to the house to connect the new wire to the original first-attachment hook.

I've placed my step ladder just below the eave area right above the interface box.

As I begin to ascend the ladder to make the hook connection, I glance back in time to see Mama pull the chain off the doghouse and start running my way.

In the moment I thought, "I'm on a ladder she can't come up he-eeeerrreee?!"

The next split second I spent continuing up the ladder and clear up onto the roof, grateful the roof eave was low.

That pissed off Mama was following me up the ladder. Just when I was sure we were going to duke it out on the roof on that house, the customer caught the dog chain and pulled the enraged Setter off the ladder.

The customer put her in the house. I collected my wits, fired up a smoke, and finished up the job.

Moral of the story?

If Mama ain't happy, ain't nobody happy.

CURIOUS A.F.

On this day, I was working out in the rural area. My customer lived on several acres and had cattle, a couple of horses, two or three dogs, and a Mama cat who had given birth to several adorable little kittens. They were old enough to run around, playing with each other and getting underfoot.

There were three who were like the Musketeers, wherever one went, the other two followed, and as I knelt on the floor working on a jack, they pawed at my wiring and any tool I laid down.

I had to climb the pole, as it was a new line I was installing, so I let my customer know I'd be working outside for a bit and went to my truck to put on my climbing gear.

I laid out the aerial service wire from the house to the pole, threaded it through my quick-release snap (in case the wire got caught on something it would pull out of the clip and not yank me off the pole), and proceeded to climb up to the terminal. I had just belted on and was opening up the terminal when I saw the limbs in the tree next to the pole were moving.

Typically, it's only squirrels jumping from limb to limb as they make their way through the trees. But these weren't squirrels.

As I peered through the leaves and branches I saw, to my amazement, that the same three little kittens who had been frolicking through the house had followed me outside and were now climbing up the tree.

Cautious but steady they came until the leader gingerly stepped on a branch at my eye level that spanned the distance between the tree and where I was on the pole. I realized he was trying to come to me, making little-meowing noises as he set one paw down and tested the branch. It was a slender branch and it bent as the kitten began to put his weight on it.

"No, no little kitty," I said firmly. I didn't want to scare them, but I also didn't want any kitten deaths on my conscience. I could just see them free falling the twenty-five feet to the ground below.

I wondered briefly if they'd land on their feet, then shook my head and snapped out of it.

I took one of my screwdrivers and banged it against the strand. The kitten closest to me—I decide to call him Athos, and the other two are Porthos and Aramis—looked up at me and stopped where he was. He started to put his paw on the branch again, and, again, I hit my screwdriver against the strand. He hesitated, and we did that little dance while I connected the service wire to the cable pair.

I was done in a couple of minutes and ready to descend the pole, but I was worried that Athos would still try to cross on the branch. So, I climbed down one step, paused and called to the three of them, took another step down and called again. It was taking me longer to climb down the pole than to do anything else on this job so far! About halfway down I heard my customer below me.

"Who are you talking to?" She was smiling and looking just a wee bit concerned.

"The kittens followed me up the pole! They're in the tree, and I'm trying to get them to come down."

At that moment she sees them, lets out a cry, and immediately begins calling them. At the familiar sound of her voice, they turn their attention to her and the lowest one in the tree starts to climb down. I hope the other two will follow, and, after a couple of seconds, they do, picking their way through the limbs; finally, they scamper down to the ground safely. I climb down the rest of the way and kneel to rub their soft heads when they rub against my leg.

"I'm glad you came out here when you did!"

"So am I!" she says. "Did I hear you say Athos or am I imagining things?" Then she tells me she used to teach literature in high school before she retired.

I smiled sheepishly and admitted that I'd named them after the Three Musketeers.

She tilted her head to one side, smiled and said, "I like that. I think you just named them for me".

OUTWIT, OUTRUN, OUT OF BREATH

I was on the west side of the city, working in an affluent neighborhood - nice houses, big yards backing up to the golf course of the country club. It was the middle of a summer afternoon, and no one was home. I walked around the side of the house to where the gate was located. There was a four-foot chain link fence all around the enormous yard, and under a big tree halfway to the fence line was a doghouse. Then I saw a couple of dog toys in the yard.

OK, I needed to make some noise. I rattled the gate and whistled. I yelled and whistled and rattled again. I unlatched the gate and stepped in, whistling again, then shut the gate. I needed to get to the interface on the back of the house, so I could isolate my trouble.

I scanned the yard as I walked, then looked around to the back of the house. I saw my interface, and I was about fifty feet away from it when, out of the corner of my left eye, I saw movement. I stopped in my tracks.

That's all it was, a brief movement. It was shady back there, with old trees covering most of the yard and house acting as a natural canopy from the midday sun. It was like a shadow had moved.

I looked in the direction I saw the movement come from, but I couldn't see anything. It was completely still. I took two steps, and I heard a low, throaty growl. I stopped breathing, and the hair on the back of my neck stood up. It sounded like the growl of a very large dog.

This happened in the space of a few seconds in real time, but, in my mind, it was all in slow motion.

As my eyes focused, I saw the shape of a large dog, eighty or ninety pounds, and I recognized the distinctive outline of his body and head. It was a German Shepherd and, as it happens, I owned one myself, so I know how protective they are. I know how smart they are. I know how fast they are.

I swear I must have leaped sideways six feet and hit the ground running. I ran straight to the fence line on sheer fear and adrenaline. I remember my tools flying out of my tool belt and hitting the fence in some mangled version of a vault while flinging myself over it.

I landed on my feet, but my momentum made me pitch backwards, landing on my butt with a jolt. I winced as I felt a twinge in my left ankle.

I looked up, and the shepherd was standing up, his feet on the top rail of the fence just looking at me. He wasn't barking. He wasn't even out of breath.

In fact, he looked rather pleased with himself. We both knew he could clear that fence in a heartbeat. It's highly probable he allowed me to reach the fence first. He sat down then and watched me. He was beautiful. Classic black and tan, muscled and proud looking. He'd done his job.

I stood up slowly, minding my sore ankle and took an inventory of how many tools I'd lost. I could see some of them in the grass, marking the exact path of my escape. I would have to leave the customer a note explaining why they didn't have phone service yet and inquire if I could come by to pick up my tools and finish the job in the morning.

"You're a smart boy, aren't you?" I said admiringly, "just waiting for me until I got all the way in the yard."

He laid down then as if to say, "I'm still waiting," and watched me as I limped back to my truck, outwitted by man's best friend.

FOR THE LOVE OF FUR

Cats and dogs, as we all know, are diametrically opposed creatures. I am neither a cat person nor a dog person. I am a primate that feeds the cats and dogs near my cave entrance, so those creatures will claim that territory as their own, thus serving as watch animals to keep vermin and other predators, whether animal or human, at bay.

No, I don't say my pets are my children, and I don't care one way or another if you do. I'm sure we understand one another now: one of us is a pet person and the other a Neanderthal.

Therefore, we can continue in sharing stories of the cute, wacky, scary, gross, violent and, at the very least, completely unexpected scenarios to which animals, in general, have subjected us humans. May I proceed?

Husky, Malamute, Akita, Samoyed, Czech Wolfdog, Kugsha, Eskimo, Inuit, Utonagan and any mutt thereof are in general, great dogs. Please allow me to clarify "great dogs." They may very well NOT be great pets. By pet, I mean the pet you got because you thought it would be cool to have a pet. Remember the goldfish you could not keep alive?

So now the Husky-like thing in the house or yard is locked up, locked in, tied down, or fenced in. You are at work, on vacation, hung over, or all the above, hanging out with your pack of other Neanderthals.

The canine, on the other hand, whose very nature is to run like hell in cold climates, chasing after anything that is small enough to fit in its hungry jaw, has indeed, in your absence, ripped the shit out of the couch.

Additionally, the dog has destroyed the curtains and everything you were dumb enough to leave on the counter. It has torn the dog food bag open, eaten all it could till it puked, scratched the door long enough to tear the doorknob off and is now in the yard ... with me.

Animals, alone with a stranger, can and will go from one extreme to the other as far as their chosen disposition.

For instance, if you leave your dog alone a lot, they may be very protective of the domicile. Case in point: there is a particular, main-cable cross box in one of our older neighborhoods. This box has folding doors that open out and lean into the chain-link fence of an adjacent yard. The mutant German-Boxer that resides in this yard is the most psychotic, evil, and sneaky dog I've ever encountered.

Every time any techs came and worked in this small cross box, that mutant would stealth his way across the length of the yard, get right up to the fence, now less than two feet away, and let out a horrid, loud barking rant. He would never friendly-up, even when given dog treats.

We all knew he was there, and, yet, every time we worked there, that SOB startled us all.

On the other hand, a lonely dog can be a loving dog to an extreme. In this scenario, she just needed some snuggling.

I was sitting on my short sit-down-tool-box working on the network interface at the back of the house. "Snuggles," a rather "husky" Husky, comes out to visit. She is home alone and wants attention.

"Hi, girl."

Over she comes, tail wagging. She walks right up and sticks her nose and face in between me and my working task.

I give her a scratch, rub, hug and a couple of "Good girl" comments, then push her away so as to work. Oh no, we're not done. She pushes back in for more. I give a bit more love and push away again. Again, she pushes all the way in, full body straddling the toolbox.

I grab a stick nearby, toss it away to distract her, push her off my lap, and she goes for the stick. The fetch game usually suffices with most dogs. Not with Snuggles, I'm afraid. No, she's like the date that does not settle for one goodnight kiss.

Snuggles returns with the stick, shoves her way between me and the house, bowls me over off my sit-box and proceeds to lay on me. Now I'm laughing and getting annoyed at the same time. She really is a very sweet, but massive dog.

So, I get up, sit back on the box, and turn my back toward her to block attempts to squeeze into my lap. I have to do this, many times, as she goes to the other side and back again while I am trying to finish my wiring repair. It really was hilarious and sad that this beautiful animal was so lonely.

After my repair work, I played a few more rounds of fetch and then made my escape from the backyard.

May I share a perspective?

Never abandon your companion.

They'll either go psycho on you and everyone else or go down on anyone else, if you get my meaning.

HEY LADY, DID YOU LOSE YOUR CAT?

One of the challenges of being a telephone technician was always, "How do I get the dial tone from point A to point B?" The customer's questions were pretty much along the lines of: "How much wiring will show? Will you have to drill a hole? How long will it take? Why does the phone wire have to show but the television cable isn't?" (Because you had the television cable installed while the room was being built and apparently the phone lines were just an afterthought.)

Sometimes, in the course of our work, we discovered information that it's very possible our customers did not, or would not, want to know about.

I am asking the woman whose house I am at where her crawl space entrance is. Firstly, she didn't know she had a crawl space. Secondly, she wasn't sure exactly what a crawl space was. And thirdly, she did not know where this entrance would be since it was in an area of her house she didn't know existed.

"OK ma'am, let me look around and I'll find it. The entrance will be outside, in the garage or sometimes it's an opening in the floor of a closet." At this, the woman's eyes got bigger and she remembered another worker, a plumber, using the closet of her spare bedroom to "do some work."

There it was, partially hidden under boxes of storage. I cleared enough space to lift out the door and shine my flashlight into the darkness. Once in a great while, some kind soul would install lighting underneath the crawl space. This was not the case here.

I'd already drilled a hole and fed down several feet of wire, so it was a matter of getting my bearings and crawling towards where I believed the wire would be. This was always interesting because, quite often, the layout of the crawl space doesn't mirror the floor plan, and I've gotten turned around under there.

This crawl space was pretty low, no room to even get up on my knees and elbows. It was belly crawl all the way. I have never been claustrophobic, but sometimes I would think about, "What if the floor collapses? Are those a pair of eyes looking at me from that corner? Oh my god, do they have a sewer pipe broken down here?" Stuff like that.

So, I am crawling along, my face inches from the earth, pushing through spider webs and broken glass and damp spots that I'd rather not know the origin of, when I see my wiring exactly where I thought it would be. Yes! I'm halfway there, pulling the wire towards a small opening on the outside wall of the crawl space. I can see daylight coming in through the opening, enough space to push my wire through when I look down right in front of me and...

Sweet Hey Zeus!! My head jerks up, banging against the floor joist and sending trails of light across my vision for a few seconds. Directly in front of me, in perfect condition and every piece in place, is the skeleton of a cat. A house cat. HER house cat that probably disappeared god knows how many years ago. Because these bones are white and dry and there is no smell whatsoever, and you know this had to smell at some point. I mean, you know this smelled BAD. How did she not know there was a dead animal under here? Or ... did she know? And is she nailing the door in the floor shut right now? I WILL DIE DOWN HERE. Ok, ok, calm down.

Calm down. Take a deep, dusty breath and get this wire out the side of the house and GET THE HELL OUT OF HERE. I crawl around the skeleton, feed my wire outside, dodge the Dead Kitty again, and head back towards the closet.

Thank God, I can see the light from the closet, so she hasn't nailed me in.

By this point, I realize there is no way I'm even mentioning the cat. No way. If she did lose track of the cat, it would devastate her to know the cat died under the house. At least, I hope it would devastate her. Or it would embarrass her. Could she not hear it meowing under there? My God, did the poor thing starve to death? How long would that have taken? What kind of a monster is this woman? There could be dead babies buried under here ...

DEAR LORD OF THE DEAD CRAWL SPACE KITTIES LET ME GET THIS JOB DONE AND GET OUT OF HERE!

And so, I did. I kept my mouth shut about the bones. I kept my eye on my customer, waiting for any signs of psychotic rage or murderous intent. She wore the mask of normalcy well. I lived to see another day, the awful secret of that dark and sinister crawl space kept safe between myself and... the One Left Behind.

OHHH, HOW CUTE IS THAT?

So, I'm up another pole in someone's blind-alley backyard.
Caution: RANT ALERT! (Note: A "blind-alley" is a utility easement area
between property lines of house lots. This area is where not only your
phone landline cables go to and come from, but also your sewer, the
water service, the electric service, the cable TV, as well as any other
crap from the city and county. This area is NOT for you or your moron
neighbor to place anything illegally in the UTILITY easement.

This is NOT your yard, NOT your property. It belongs to the county
you pay your property taxes to. A long time ago, the city and county
cheapen out on the responsibility of paving, graveling or even mowing
this area, thus leaving the opportunity for the developers to let you
believe the 20-foot-wide COUNTY Utility easement belongs to you and
your neighbor.

Well, it does not. If it did, you could lease that area to the power
company, the CATV company, the telephone company, etc. BUT, you
can't, can you? Huh? Why not? Because it would be illegal! That
property is PUBLICLY owned!

YET ... you have set your fence, your shed, your landscaping, your
fucking smelly-ass dog pen, and yet another valuable antique piece of

crap Edsel not only on top of the easement but up against the pole or worse, OVER the buried telco cable pedestal-terminal I need to get to in order to repair your neighbor's internet service, so they may get back to online gambling. But, noooooo ... I have to climb over, up, and around the crap YOU are storing and placing illegally just to do my job. That easement is MY domain, get it?! So, YOU ... NOW ... go get that junk out of my way ... Whew ... ahem ... thanks.

OK ... Back to the cute story.

So, I'm on this pole on a pleasant sunny day. A perfect example of why I loved this job. No, really, I did.

I'm done repairing the drop wire and am closing the terminal door when I hear a low-volume, high pitch kind of squeal near my right ear. It did not startle me, just slightly surprised and intrigued me at the same time. I slowly looked over my shoulder.

At first, I did not know what I was looking at or for. My focus was several feet away.

Then, as I heard it again, I saw, about 2 feet away, on a small branch, level with my head, something very small, say, the size of a mouse.

Hanging upside-down was a little, tiny ... bat.

It was slightly spreading its wings while yawning and made the same squeal sound. It folded itself back up into its wings like a cocoon.

As I reached over and gently stroked the length of the cocoon, it shuddered, squealed a bit more, and closed up again.

How cute is that?

I must admit, that alone was worth climbing over that damned Edsel.

PIT BULL GAUNTLET

This trouble report was in a lower income neighborhood, one with working-class families. Most of the houses were rentals in various stages of deterioration; the houses needed painting, porch railings were busted, windows were cracked with bars on them, trash littered the yards along with detritus from old appliances and vehicles. My report indicated this customer's trouble was in the overhead line servicing his house. "How do we know that?" you might ask. Our central office test equipment became more and more sophisticated as technology improved.

We test a line to see what type of trouble is present. If it's intermittent it can drive you a little crazy, while other types of trouble are easier to isolate. Our equipment could measure the distance of an open in a line within a few feet. Now, this wasn't always 100% accurate, but it sure narrowed our search down and gave us somewhere to start isolating the trouble.

My test said the line was open approximately 150 feet from the house. This is probably a squirrel-chewed line at the pole, a very common issue, and it's an easy fix—simply replace the line.

If I haven't said it already, squirrels were job security. Something about the neoprene and the copper wire is irresistible to them, and you could see the little teeth marks on the line and the broken, corroded copper that had been exposed to the elements, thanks to our little rodent friends.

In this case though, first I had to get to the pole.

When I step into the backyard, I see a narrow path leading from the back steps to the fence at the rear of the property where my pole is. It's obvious this is the path the owners walk when they come out to feed the two pit bulls that are chained on opposite sides of the yard.

Each dog is straining at the end of the thick chain holding him, running full speed until he is yanked off his feet. Their mouths are foaming. They reach either side of the narrow path and are stopped just short of being able to reach the middle. These dogs are in a frenzy as they watch me, and I'm absolutely certain they will rip me to pieces if I walk between them.

"You can go ahead and walk out there. They can't reach you," my customer says to me when I tell him I need to get to the pole. "I feed them every day. They ain't going to hurt you," he says with a grin that makes me think the exact opposite.

"I am not walking between those two dogs. You need to put them up, so I can replace this overhead line." I am looking at this customer with an expression on my face that says I AM NOT KIDDING. "Where am I supposed to put them? You see a garage around here? Hey, maybe I can put them in their private kennels. How about that? Shit. I ain't moving them." And he goes back inside the house. I am tempted at this point to just leave but I know it would only fall to another technician to do this and I cannot do that.

OK, there has to be a way.

I pay out enough aerial service wire to reach the pole from the

84

house. I cut down the old wire from the house and tie the new line to the old one. I hook up the other end of the service wire to the attachment on the house, then run it into the interface and terminate it on the protector.

I clean up and let my customer know I'm driving around the block to get to the pole from his neighbor's yard behind him. I throw my extension ladder up over the six-foot wooden fence and lean it against my pole.

Once up on the pole, I pull the damaged line down and use it to pull up my new service wire. I watch the dogs as they snap at the line when I pull it through the yard, praying one of them doesn't get hold of it in his teeth.

Jeez, they are literally jumping up in the air as I raise the line above their heads. It looks like some macabre dance, the pit bulls leaping into the air at the wire, foam spraying from their mouths, their muscular bodies twisting as they jump. I do not want to know whether this customer may be using these as fighting dogs, or if he is just another person who really does not deserve to own animals.

Whatever reason he may have for treating his dogs like this was not okay with me. I will say that they had plenty of water, and they were fed. No shelter other than the shade from the trees, but not enough visible evidence that would have me call and report this.

I take a deep breath, finish up, and call my customer from the pole. We can hardly hear one another over his dogs barking, but he knows his service is repaired. He is saying, "I told you I wouldn't have to move my damn dogs," when I hang up my headset.

Oops.

He comes out on his back porch while I am climbing down my ladder. He's yelling at me, and, fortunately, I can't hear a word he's saying because of the dogs. How ironic. I stop halfway down and notice he isn't walking down that narrow path between the dogs, now is he? I beckon him to come on, I motion for him to walk on down that path to the bottom of the pole and that's when he gives me the finger. That's when I distinctly see the words FUCK YOU form on his lips, more than once.

I am even gladder at that moment to be on the other side of the six-foot fence that separates the two yards, the two pit bulls, and a customer who refuses to walk the gauntlet between his own dogs. Oh, and you're welcome for fixing your phone line.

TECHNICIAN POETRY

Rural area ...

Dirt road ...

Buried cable ...

Open out ... (broken wire in laymen's terms)

Piece of cake ...

Beautiful day ...

Dry and high 70s ...

There's the pedestal ...

Nice ... no water in ditch ...

Pedestal on this side of barb-wire fence ...

Pedestal in good condition ...

Easy to work on and at ...

Tall grass in ditch, just not at my ped ...

Did I mention NICE?

Sit-down-box, nice and comfy ...

Wire connections at eye-level ...

This is a day when I should be paying them to work here ...

Brain comfy and secure ...

Lulled into false security ...

Loud rustle to the right ...

Startled glance ...

Tall grass shaking violently ...

WHAT THE FUCK IS THA ...

A coyote, cougar???

AAAAAhhhh ...

oh, shiiitttt....

OooOOOOOo...

Oh, you little shit...

scared me half to death....

niiice doggy

(slobbering all over me)...

INSANE SHIT I DID IN MY TRUCK

You may not realize this, but I have a temper. Surprising, I know. Especially when someone is being condescending or a bully, my tendency is to draw a line in the sand and dare them to cross it.

I was working out in a rural area north of the city. All our facilities were underground, so I was kneeling down in a ditch working at a pedestal and on the phone with our test center. I was not paying attention to anything going on around me because I was so intent on fixing the trouble I was dispatched for, but eventually, the sound of an idling engine reached my brain.

I turned around, and behind my truck was an older guy, the proverbial John Deere ball cap on his head, sitting in a road grader, glaring at me. I shut down my test equipment and walked over to him.

"Can I help you with something?" I asked him.

"I work for the county grading these roads up here. Don't you EVER park your truck where it's blocking part of the road! You can pull down into the ditch if you need to do your work. I been waiting on you too long already."

I just stared at him for a few seconds, amazed at how angry he was and by the fact that he had the gall to tell me I couldn't park my truck on a public road in the course of doing my job. This is about the time my temper kicked in.

"Why don't you stop whining and get back in your fucking cab and do your job?"

His jaw dropped. I don't know what he thought I was going to say, but I'm pretty sure he didn't anticipate that.

"You need to move your damn phone truck."

"I'll move it when I'm done here. Pull around me." With that, I turned around and walked back to pick up my test equipment.

I heard him mumble something that ended with an emphatic, very loud "Bitch!" and then he pulled around my truck and started grading the road again.

Would that I had let it go at that, but no, I couldn't. The more I thought about it, the angrier and more indignant I became.

I put all my tools and equipment up and got in my truck. I could see him ahead of me about a half mile or so. I caught up to the road grader guy and his blatant, good old boy, misogynist attitude, and I pulled in front of him and stopped. Then I waited.

I'm watching him in my side mirror, and he's getting pretty riled up.

Just when he looked like he was going to get out, I pulled away very slowly.

He waited several seconds, then started grading, and I pulled over and stopped in front of him again. At this point, I could see the veins popping out in his neck, and I felt assuaged in a self-righteous sort of way, so I pulled away and drove into the central office in this little town to call my supervisor.

I let her know that she may be getting a call from the county, and I explained what happened. I heard her take a deep breath, and then she spoke:

"You know you're one of my best technicians," she began. "If I get a call from the county, I'll handle it. But you have got to stop putting yourself and me in this position! One of these times they're going to go above my head, and I don't know if I can help you at that point."

She was absolutely right. As much for her sake as my own (because she really was a good supervisor, and I liked working for her), I resolved to work on that.

Until the next idiot comes along who deserves it.

Driving a Ma Bell truck for 30 years gives one perspective on other drivers. I firmly believe that when some people see a Ma Bell vehicle, they see money. As in, "I'll go ahead and pull out in front of this phone truck because I'll sue if they hit me."

I even had a guy park behind my truck while I was working in a business suite who claimed I backed into him; his hood was already kept in place by three bungee cords. I called my supervisor out to look at that one, and it was pretty clear those bungee cords had been on there for a while. He took a bunch of photographs and gave the guy our claims department number, but I never heard anything after that.

But there were other times when I let my temper and my self-righteousness take over. Like the time when this man pulled out in front of me, and I had to slam on my brakes to keep from hitting him.

I laid on the horn, and when I did, the guy gave me the finger. Well, that was all it took. I followed him several miles from where I had been going until he stopped at a house and walked in the back door.

I pulled up his address in my computer, and he had two lines working in his house. Not for long. I drove to the cross box that serves his neighborhood and disconnected both lines into this guy's house.

Was it a childish thing to do? Probably. Do I regret doing it? Nope. Would I do that again today? Of course not ... I think.

Another time I was driving on an access road where there was construction going on in the field next to it. One lane was closed, and there was a guy standing between a couple of trucks holding a sign - the kind that says, "Stop," on one side and, "Slow," on the other.

It said "Stop," and so I did, but there wasn't any oncoming traffic. I waited one or two minutes then eased up to the sign holder slowly. He was talking with a construction worker and didn't turn around.

"Hey," I shouted through the passenger window.

"There's no traffic. I'm going on through here".

At this, he turns around, and I can see he is irritated.

"Go on then. What are you waiting for?" he snarls at me. He angrily motions me to go forward.

"Hey, you're holding the sign! Do your job!" I yell as I'm starting to pull out.

Now he's mad and he says, "Get the fuck out of here! Get your fucking truck out of here!"

So, naturally, I stop.

"Fuck you, motherfucker!" I yell and hit the gas.

Looking in my mirror, I see him throw down the sign and get into one of the trucks. Holy shit! He's coming after me!

I am about four minutes from the work location where we park our trucks, get supplies, and have our offices for this area. If I can make it there even one minute ahead of him and pull in next to the other trucks, he won't know which one mine is, unless he got the number from the back. I am fervently hoping he was not in the frame of mind to do that.

I pull in and park next to one of the cable repairmen on my crew, one of my buddies, so I know he'll be in the office. I fly out of the cab and run into the office about twenty feet away. No sign of this guy, yet. I slam open the door to the office and startle my buddy, Dennis.

"Jesus, what the hell are you doing?"

"I'm going into the bathroom. If a construction guy comes in here looking for me, you never saw me." With that, I go through another door into the adjoining women's restroom. I lock the door and wait for a minute. Then two, then three, then Dennis knocks on the door.

"I think it's safe for you to come out. He ain't coming in here looking for you," he says through the door. I open the door and step out, looking at the vehicles parked inside the garage. Then I thanked Dennis for being my lookout. He just shook his head and smiled.

At this point, I'd like to point out that I was much younger and far less wise back in those days. I grew up working for Ma Bell, literally from 18 years old to age 48 when I retired.

This next story demonstrates that we were almost too resourceful for our own good. Just because you think of a way to do something you thought was impossible doesn't mean you actually have to try it.

A crew of between four and six of us, depending on the workload, were pre-wiring an apartment complex. While it's being built, all the different contractors install their wiring, vents, and plumbing before the walls are sheet-rocked. So that's what we're doing, pre-wiring our first building when we all realize none of our ladders will reach high enough on the building to finish the job and run the wire to the mechanical room.

We had the longest ladders we used, at 28 feet fully extended, and they were about eight feet short. We could call for a bucket truck but a) it wouldn't necessarily be available and b) whether it's available or not, then someone else in the company knows why we wanted it. Then one of us, I truly don't remember who, but someone proposed that if we put the ladder on TOP of the van, then it would reach.

Here's the thing: it was absolutely doable but off the fucking chart stupid in the job safety department.

So, we all agreed to do it.

We pulled the van alongside the building, and one of the guys got on top of the van and placed the ladder against the building. It reached where we needed it to go. Son of a bitch! This was going to work.

One of us drove to the entrance of the complex to look out for supervisors or other technicians. So, three of us were on top of the van; one would climb, while the other two held the ladder. We agreed that we'd take turns climbing. We got both buildings finished that day.

It wasn't that bad being up on the ladder that day if you could forget about the fact that it was on top of a van where two of your co-workers stood holding it steady. If you could not think about the kind of trouble if not outright dismissal this would bring if anyone saw and/or reported us. If you refused to think that one of us could get seriously injured or worse. Youth and ignorance, a volatile combination.

I was working north of the city, out in the country where I had to run an aerial service wire five spans. (A span is the distance between two poles.) This means I climbed a total of six poles to get service to this house.

It was summer, and it was hot and humid. Now, all the technicians carried a five-gallon water bucket on our trucks, and we'd fill them fresh every morning. It wasn't unusual for me to drink most of that, especially working 10-hour days.

For this particular job, my customer didn't have to be home since all my work was outside. I'd been drinking water all day and sweating it out just as quickly as I drank it.

There were no trees, no shade and no air conditioning in my truck. (I would not drive a truck with air conditioning until the last five years of my thirty years with the company.)

I had just climbed up the last pole and attached my service wire when my vision got blurry, and I felt light-headed. I was belted in, so I leaned back in my safety belt and closed my eyes for about thirty seconds, willing my vision to be clear again. It worked, but I was still light-headed, and my heart was pounding. I was sweating profusely and felt a little nauseous, so I knew it was probably heat exhaustion. I knew I needed to get off the pole and into some shade pretty quickly.

I started climbing down the pole, still belted in. Most times I descended without being belted in; we are taught a three-point contact method when climbing, but given my condition, I didn't want to take any chances of falling off the pole completely.

My legs were shaky as I climbed down, and I just kept thinking, "One step closer to the ground. One more step."

Once both feet were on solid ground, I unbelted and walked to my truck. I took off my climbing belt, my hooks (what we wore on our legs to climb the pole), and my tool belt and filled a water bottle with ice-cold water.

I dropped to my knees and crawled under my truck, the only shade available. I laid there for about twenty minutes or so, sipping water and listening to my heartbeat slow down. Once I was sure I could finish the job, I crawled out from under my truck, drove up to the house, and completed the installation.

Now mind you, this was before cell phones. We carried pagers, and, if we needed to call someone, we climbed a pole or opened up a terminal fed by underground cable and got on someone's dial tone to make that call. This was somewhat surprising to people, understandably, if they went to use their phone and someone from the phone company was talking on it.

Most people were patient and would hang up and let me finish my business, but there were a few people who launched into the same diatribe every time:

"I'm paying for this phone line. What are you doing talking on it"?

To which I would reply, "We are working on the lines in this area and will be off your phone line in just a few minutes."

Usually, at that point, they hang up, but if they don't—and sometimes people would just refuse to hang up—I would disconnect them myself until I was done with the call. Because it IS Ma Bell's dial tone and you ARE just renting it from us.

AT THE AIRFORCE BASE
(OR HOW TO GET ARRESTED WITHOUT REALLY TRYING)

I worked with some characters at Ma Bell. One of my co-workers was the son of an upper management supervisor. When I say upper management, I mean this is the guy who could actually fire you. Now, his son, Jerry, liked to have a good time, and he also liked to push the boundaries whenever possible.

On this particular day, we were out at the Air Force Base to install a couple of pay phones in one of the hangars.

There is a strict procedure to follow when working at a military facility. The Military Police check our vehicles and have the drug/weapons dogs sniff all around. You have to go into an office where they take your IDs, see if you are on the list to be allowed on base, and issue visitor passes.

So, the MP's take us into what is essentially a hallway. There are two-way mirrors on both sides of the hall, so presumably, someone is in there watching us. There's an office at the end of the hall but there is—and this is important—a red line on the floor in front of us, with bold letters that say, "STAND BEHIND THIS LINE. DO NOT CROSS."

Pretty clear, don't you think? Not a whole lot of room for misinterpretation.

We've been standing in this hallway for a few minutes when Jerry gets this look on his face that I know means trouble.

"Dare me to step over this line?" he asks with an ornery grin.

"Don't. They'll be out in a minute, just wait."

"No, really. What do you think would happen?"

"I don't know, and I don't want to find out."

I shake my head at him. This is partly true. The grown up in me, the small voice of reason screaming in my head is saying, 'Don't be an idiot.' It's also pointing out that we are the only ones in this building who are not carrying weapons.

However, the little kid in me is saying, 'Go ahead, Jerry. Do it!'

So, he walks up to the line, grinning like a lunatic, sticks one foot over and then steps back, like an insane version of the hokey pokey.

Both doors on either side of the hallway burst open immediately, and there are two MPs with guns drawn filling both doorways.

They are not amused. Without even realizing it, I have my hands up, my eyes on the handgun the airman closest to me have pointed at my partner.

Jerry is trying, unsuccessfully, to make light of what he did. They tell him to stop talking. They tell me to stay where I am. One of the MPs escorts Jerry into the office behind him.

After what seems like an eternity, an airman comes out with a visitor's pass for me and tells me I can proceed with my work order. I ask him about my partner, and he says he will be delayed for a while longer.

I thank him and leave the office, go out to my truck and wait. And wait.

Twenty minutes go by, and my pager goes off. It's our immediate supervisor. I call him from the cross box, and he is incredulous when I verify what has happened.

He has just gotten a call from HIS supervisor, who just got a call from HIS supervisor who happens to be—you guessed it—Jerry's dad. Jerry's little prank—and it is now officially a "security breach"—has gotten the attention of upper management and everyone in between. Jerry is being escorted out to his truck.

"They called all the way up to my dad," he says sheepishly, "to verify who I am."

"Oh, they know who you are now, alright. So, are they letting you stay"?

"Yeah. My old man talked to the officer in charge back there and we can finish the job."

He looks at me for a moment, "Why'd you let me do that?" he asks, only half kidding. "If there's ever another incident I'll be banned from the base," he informs me.

"That's understandable. You know if your dad wasn't a third line supervisor, we'd both probably be banned. Let's get to work."
Jeez.

OH, THE THINGS WE ALMOST DO

I'm on a repair ticket called in two days prior, and it is a hot summer day. It's about three o'clock, and I knock on the door of the apartment. This is a brick building, four apartments on ground level, and I have to run a wire around most of the building to fix the line.

The original wire had pulled away from the brick and was lying close enough to the ground that it got clipped by the weed trimmer. I decide to run the new wire along the wood trim under the eaves, up high and far from any lawn implements.

My customer is a guy around my age, in his thirties, and it turns out he is an electrician as well as a musician. So, we have some things in common, and once I'm back in the house, drenched in sweat and grateful to be out of the heat, we start talking about music and it turns out we like a lot of the same artists.

As we're talking, the customer asks if it would be too much trouble to move the jack to the other side of the couch, and I tell him no problem. It's maybe fifteen feet, and so we both get hold of each end of the couch and heave it out from the wall.

There on the floor sits the proverbial drive-in tray. Some of you may not remember, but certain drive-in hamburger chains would bring your food on a tray that was made to hang on the driver's side window.

This tray was also perfect for cleaning the seeds and stems from your weed and for rolling joints. I worked at a drive-in all through high school, and I cannot tell you how many times those trays were stolen. In fact, drive-ins no longer use those trays, and I think it's in no small way related to dope rolling thievery.

But I digress.

On the stolen drive-in tray sits at least an ounce of what looks to be some damn good pot. Some rolling papers (the orange ones, for all of you willing to admit you know exactly what I'm talking about), and a couple of lighters.

"Oh shit!" my customer says when he sees the tray. "I forgot about that being there. Let me get that out of your way," and he picks up the tray.

"It's cool," I tell him with a knowing look. "Don't worry about me."

He cocks his head slightly and asks, "You get high?"

"Well, I have been known to do that, yes," I say with a smile.

"You want to smoke one with me before you go?" he grins at me like he knows I'm going to say yes.

Which I seriously consider doing.

As I finish running the wire he sets the tray across his knees and proceeds to roll a joint. I clean up my work area and take all my tools and material out to the truck, and I stand there for a minute, running this scenario through my very-much-leaning-toward-doing-this mind.

This is my last ticket of the day. I'll go home after this.

In my head, we sit on the couch and smoke and talk for a few more minutes. I imagine we say goodbye and I step out into the

101

blazing afternoon sun. It's at this point I snap out of it and realize I wouldn't make it from the apartment to my truck in this heat if I were to choose to partake. I walk back up to the door, step in and thank my customer for his offer but politely decline. He shrugs his shoulders, smiles, and tells me to stop back by sometime when I'm not working. Hmmm...

Ah, the kindness of strangers.

REPAIRING A PARTY LINE

I am dating myself, aren't I? Party lines were when anywhere from two to eight people shared the line, shared that same pair of copper wires from the central office all the way into their homes.

Each party was assigned a position with their own special ringtone. It might be one long, one short for the Smiths, and for their neighbor down the road it was two long rings, and so on.

Also, it was on the honor system because any one of the people who were on the party line could pick up the phone at any time, just like it was an extension phone in their own house. Same thing, just different houses.

There was a certain amount of courtesy and patience necessary for everyone to get along.

In order for each party to have their own distinctive ring that was assigned to them, all the phones in the house had to be wired a specific way internally. As an installer, that meant it was my job to rewire all the sets in the house and make sure they all rang on that position and not when someone else's position was supposed to ring.

You can imagine the confusion if there are eight different households on a party line and all the damn phones are ringing at once. Or not ringing at all. Everything had to be exactly right for this to work, and one of the most important aspects of how the party line worked was the ground wire.

This was something every single line ever installed had to have—a ground.

It is, first and foremost, a safety issue to protect our equipment and, of course, our customer from power surges or electrocution. It provides somewhere for that current—be it from a lightning strike to equipment failure to human error—to go, safely, and hopefully not cause any damage or injury.

So it is imperative that the equipment be grounded, and the best, safest way is to ground everything to a common source.

First choice was always the ground that the electrical box is grounded to. However, that is not always possible given the construction of the house - especially in older homes where these specifications weren't in place when they were built.

This was the case on the repair ticket I had been dispatched on. I was still pretty new and had not worked on party lines much at all, so Jerry was with me to teach me.

The report was 'bells don't ring on party line." Ok, I did know that the first thing we check is the ground wire, and no, it wasn't grounded. The number 10-gauge copper wire going from our protector to the ground rod at the corner of the house was intact and connected to the ground rod, but it still isn't grounded.

'How is this even possible?' is what I'm thinking as I stand there looking at the ground rod. Jerry is standing next to me and asks me what I think.

"I don't know what to think. It's connected to the ground rod, so how can it not be grounded?"

Jerry smiles and says, "It's been a while since we've had any rain. Look how dry it is."

He walks over to the ground rod and nudges it with his boot. It moves around too easily. As he moves it, I'm watching my test equipment and the needle pops up for a second, indicating a ground is present. Then it's gone.

Jerry turns his back to me and is facing the field in back of the house, standing over the ground rod.

"Watch and learn. This is called creative repair." He unzips his jeans and proceeds to urinate on the ground rod.

I am speechless and appalled. He finishes and is walking back to the house while I am scrambling to get my equipment and close up the interface. I hear the phones ringing as I am walking to my truck, and Jerry leaves the house shortly after.

Ok, I think, the phones are working for now.

"Jerry, the same thing is going to happen when it dries up again!"

"Don't worry. I told them to turn the water hose on it next time." He's laughing and gets in his truck to leave.

I tell him I left a tool at the back of the house and watch as he drives off. Then I do something that would serve me well over many years; I trust my own instincts.

I return to the protector and run a new ground wire to the common ground where the electrical equipment is grounded to. It takes some work because it is halfway around the house, but it's the right thing to do. I let the customer know what I did, and I tell them their phone will work, rain or no rain.

And silently I think, "Pee or no pee."

ROTTEN THINGS

There are myriads of things that decompose. Often times they are discovered at damned inconvenient times. You know, like when you've poured the spoiled milk on the last bowl of cereal or into a fresh cup-o-java. You just want to cry or kill, right?

Well, sometimes the "rot" will try to kill you.

Lots of cities have blind alleys. You've likely already read my rant that this is NOT your property, so I shall proceed to the point of this individual scenario.

Some residential areas with blind alleys have enough property space between the house and the utility easement to add an entire other house and yard. In this particular area, these lots are 200-plus-feet deep to the aerial utility poles. Adding to the issue, this is an 80-year-old neighborhood. This means that damn few folks here mow or trim anything. So, I'm traversing a football field deep jungle.

I manage to snake through the dead cars, with new tree lines growing through the hood of said dead auto to inspect the easement and decide how to climb the foliage-overgrown pole.

"Well, at least this piece of crap has pole-steps," I reassure myself. I return to the truck, get all belted on, tool pouch belted on, and I also grab the end of a new aerial wire to drag back to the terminal. Might as well upgrade the wire since I'm already going through the pain-in-the-ass to get back there anyway.

After the backyard hike, I proceed up the pole while simultaneously hacking off several tree branches that have been growing around the pole and the terminal at the top. After much jungle-machete work, I get myself belted on and situated to work on the terminal enclosure.

As I'm tracing which drop wire in this rat's nest of wires is mine, I move up, down and sideways on the pole steps. I begin to feel as if I'm swaying a little too much. I quickly realize my lower extremities are moving forward and backward. This is not correct.

When one is standing on the pole steps of a utility pole, you do not swing forward and backward. This is because the pole does not move. Unless ... HOLY SHIT!

Safety lesson: Technicians are required, by company policy, to perform a list of tests on the telephone poles before ascending said pole. This policy will aid in the protection of the technician from incidents of ...

... the gawd-damn pole is rotted out and swinging from the base!

As I collect myself from this epiphany, I notice that the pole I'm on, as well as the cable and strand, are completely supported and suspended by and from the trees that have grown up, around and between the poles adjacent in both directions.

For a few moments, I was scared to death. Now I'm having fun, making the pole swing some more and listening to the creaking noise the cable strand makes in the trees.

Yeah, I'll admit it, I was the moron who blithely ignored safety protocols and then enjoyed the continuation of stupid behavior by swinging the pole to and fro. I mean, how often do you get to do silly stuff like that?

Well, in our case, lots.

THE PAYPHONE YEARS
(OR THE EASIEST THREE YEARS OF MY CAREER)

After divestiture, the landscape of telecommunications would
never be the same again.

Around this time, a crew was formed specifically to work on pay
telephones because they were still a profitable venture. The cell
phone revolution was somewhere in the future, and you couldn't pull
up to a convenience store or drive more than a couple of blocks
before you'd see a bank of payphones all lined up and in use. It was
the first choice of communication for drug dealers everywhere!!

There were four of us, two installers and two repairmen, and we
covered the entire city and surrounding areas. Our immediate
supervisor was one of the nicest guys I ever worked for, and our
second line supervisor worked out of another city entirely, so we
rarely saw him at all.

We got to choose our hours, how long we had for lunch (7:30 to
4:00 with a half hour lunch), and best of all, since we reported to a
different second line in another jurisdiction, we didn't have to answer
to anyone other than our first line boss. And we never worked
weekends. Like I said, the easiest three years of my career.

There were a few drawbacks, however, such as working in the

strip clubs and certain bars I would never have entered were it not-for, the purpose of business. Naturally, no one else on my crew (all men except for me) would consider those drawbacks. More on that later.

After several months, my buddy, Greg, and I had gotten into the habit of meeting around three o'clock every Friday at designated bars. Just to make it official, we would make up a repair ticket on the pay phone at said bar, so we'd have something to charge our time to, so we could get paid ... for drinking on company time.

It's a typical bar, with the mirror behind all the bottles running the length of the bar, so as you're sitting there, you can see what's going on behind you. We're laughing and chatting up the bartender, and we're both draining our first bottles of beer, when we notice what's going on behind us - our immediate supervisor.

He steps up between us, stands there with his hands on each of our shoulders and says:

"This is the last time this is going to happen, isn't it?"

It was not a question. It was one of the few times both Greg and I were speechless. In the next breath, our supervisor ordered a red beer, two more for us, and joined us at the bar - for the last time.

Now, let's talk about strip clubs and sex shops, kids! Had I ever been in a strip club or a sex shop prior to working in the payphone crew? No, I had not. So, this was a completely new experience for me. And it was freaking weird, let me tell you.

The first time I had a repair ticket in a sex shop, I walked in and there were two male customers watching a video on a small television screen. As I walk by, I am trying not to look at the video. I'm thinking, 'What the hell is that? Is that a body part? It's moving and ...'

Suddenly the camera backs up enough that I can make out

exactly which body parts are involved, and I'm pretty sure there was an audible gasp on my part. Yep, I recognize that now. OK, keep walking ...

I learned that there are these little booths a man can pay to go into for a private show and that the management literally swabs the booth down after each customer.

I learned that in the strip clubs the phone equipment is invariably in the dressing room (if that isn't a misnomer I don't know what is) of the dancers.

I learned that most of these women look pretty hard when they're not in the low lighting of the dance stage. Many of them are sharing a pint, passing it around, smoking cigarettes, and talking about their kids or boyfriends or exes.

I wonder what brings a woman to this place, where she makes a living like this. I am in my mid-twenties and extremely grateful to be employed by Ma Bell. I try not to judge these women, but I feel a sadness that an industry exists where women are sexualized and objectified and denigrated. Many industries. But I digress.

It was late afternoon when I was dispatched to a certain strip club out west on the highway. The aircraft plants' second shifts had just gotten off, so the club was crowded.

I wound my way through to the bar and asked for the manager.

One thing about working in a strip club is that no one pays much attention to me. I trace the trouble back outside and will need my six-foot ladder to reach the interface mounted up on the side of the building.

So, I'm up on my ladder when two guys stumble into the parking lot from inside the club. I am watching them, but they don't see me. They're lighting their cigarettes and they walk not ten feet from me to the side of the building where I'm working. They both unzip their pants and start to urinate against the building, swaying all the while. The first one speaks.

"You know that waitress in there? Who brought us our beer last time?"

"Yeah, yeah," says his buddy who has put one hand on the building to steady himself.

"She wants to fuck me so bad."

I stop myself from laughing out loud. Vanity, thou art a drunk who fancies himself a ladies' man whilst pissing in a parking lot. Because if that doesn't scream sexy, I don't know what does.

APOPLECTIC LANDLORD

I was on what should have been an easy rewire order. We had already been out to give this customer service using a temporary line we laid on the ground, and now I was there to switch the service over to the permanent line that had been buried by one of our contractors.

This was a duplex, and my customer wasn't home, but they didn't need to be. All the work was outside at our terminal, then at the house.

Once I had completed the work at the terminal (the backyard was not fenced), I went to the back of the duplex working on the interface. I was going to feed the new line through a plastic conduit, which would then be attached to the house. This way everything is uniform and looks good.

I was in the process of doing this when the guy who lives in the other half of the duplex comes out his back door.

"Why are you on my property?" he demands. I looked at his red face and could see he was upset.

"Sir, I'm working on the phone line for this side of the duplex," I responded, pointing to my customer's side. "It won't disrupt your service at all. I'll be done in a few minutes".

"I own this duplex. You're on my property. You don't have permission to be here, and you need to leave." He was getting even more red-faced and becoming angrier.

Okay. So, this is how it's going to be.

"By requesting service from Ma Bell, my customer has given me permission to be here. And just to be clear, you may own this property but this equipment" (and I gesture to the interface and the line I'm holding in my hands), "this is the property of Ma Bell. As I said, I'll be done in ... "

With that, he steps towards me. His eyes are bulging. He is an alarming shade of purple, and he is visibly shaking. I have two thoughts in quick succession:

1) He is going to hit me, and

2) If he does, I will punch him in the mouth as hard as I can, and then I'm making a run for my vehicle. But he doesn't hit me.

He grabs the underground line, yanks it from my hands, and throws it on the ground between us. I am stunned for a second. Then I pick up the line and - never taking my eyes off this raging idiot - start to feed it back through the conduit.

"I am ordering you off my property! Now!" He is in my personal space, just a few inches from me. I speak to him calmly.

"I'm not leaving my customer without phone service. Why don't you go back inside?"

He grabs the conduit out of my hands, again yanking the phone line out, and he throws the conduit halfway across the yard. I am pretty sure he's foaming at the mouth.

I have had it. I look at the line lying on the ground for the second time. I look at the guy.

"You are an asshole," I said in a low voice.

114

"I TOLD YOU TO GET THE FUCK OFF MY PROPERTY!"

"I'm calling the police."

I turn and walk to my truck. I half expect him to follow me, so I'm looking over my shoulder. By now, I've gone from angry to, 'Holy shit, this guy really is crazy.'

His aggressiveness is just over the top, unprovoked, and uncalled for. I wonder if he's on mental health meds or maybe he stopped taking them.

Once I'm in the cab, I lock the doors and call the police. Then I call my supervisor.

In just a few minutes, the supervisor is there. He had just recently been promoted to his position. Carl and I worked together as technicians, and he is shaking his head as I get out of my truck to greet him.

"Where is this guy? Did he go back inside?" he asks as he's looking towards the duplex.

"I don't know. I haven't seen him since I came out here to call you and the cops."

As if on cue, the police car pulls up. The officer comes over to speak with us.

"Which one of you called us out?"

"I did, officer. The guy I'm having trouble with lives there," I said, pointing to his side of the duplex. "My customer lives on the other side. I need to tell you that I did call this guy an asshole."

The officer doesn't respond to that, so I tell him what I was there to do and what happened with Mr. Apoplectic. Carl confirms that everything I've done is standard procedure. Well, maybe not calling someone an asshole.

The officer listens patiently and asks a few questions, then we walk around to the back of the house.

"Okay, let's see what this gentleman has to say."

The officer knocks on the back door. The man opens the door, and he has not calmed down at all. He may be even more worked up than before.

He is yelling at the officer, "I told her this is my property! I didn't ask the phone company to come out here! I want her off my property!" He's nothing if not consistent.

Very calmly, the officer asks him, "Sir, what do you do for work?"

The man is taken aback by this question. "Why do you need to know that?"

"Well, it's the middle of the day, and I was wondering if you work from home, or if you just happened to be here this afternoon," the officer answers patiently.

"I do work from home, as a matter of fact. I'm a web designer, although I don't know what that has to do with anything."

The officer nods and says, "So you work with computers, right?"

"Yes, officer. Web designers work with computers." He says this with just enough sarcasm to warrant the officer using his Taser. I am disappointed when he doesn't.

"You don't do any work with phones or phone lines?" The man shakes his head no.

The officer gestures towards me. "This woman does work with phone lines. She knows what she's doing and you're going to let her finish what she came out here to do."

Mr. Apoplectic's jaw drops open. He is, thankfully, speechless.

"You can stand out here or go back inside, but you will not approach her again. If I'm called back out here, this will not end pleasantly for you. Do we understand each other, sir?"

"Yeah, yeah, I understand. I'm going inside." He slams the door hard.

I ask Carl to stay while I finish, and he says he will. The officer tells me to call back if I need to, but he doesn't think that will be necessary.

As he walks to his vehicle, he hesitates for a second, looks at me and says, "He is an asshole, isn't he?" I get just the slightest smile from him as he opens his car door.

I thank him for coming out, and, within fifteen minutes, I am done with a job that should have taken all of forty-five minutes to complete had it not been for a home-based web designer with too much time on his hands and a lot of misdirected anger.

It feels good to be right, but it feels really good to be right and have a policeman back you up.

EXCUSE THE MESS

You've likely seen sloppy, hoarder types in houses on TV shows. We've had to dive in head first with no oxygen mask, no help from hazardous waste management, no warning from the customer, and certainly no sympathy from our own administration. That's why we're paid the big bucks.

We are always looking for clues for all potential safety hazards. Debris, pets, kids' toys, etc. that can be tripped over. However, the invisible can be a very unpleasant surprise.

One day I stepped up on the porch of a seemingly benign older bungalow that simply looked ... old. As I leaned in to ring the doorbell, the air vent from the eaves released an evil that was silent and most deadly.

Imagine something that reeks in a way that convinces you that whatever it is must be dead, yet has a life to it that was reborn from some Dante's Hell.

It was too late. I had already rung the bell. The Hades stench reached out from its innermost evil chakra and punched me in the face. As I attempted to jerk away to keep from hurling, I heard the

customer's footsteps approaching the door. It was too late. I ... I ...
(cough) could not escape.

EXCUSE THE MESS 2.0 UPGRADE

More often than not, humanity, in general, to some degree or another, tends to judge a book by the cover. I know I do. I know you do, whether you know that or not.

Basically, everyone has been in someone else's home. We have all experienced the delight of a well-appointed home that we indeed covet in some fashion.

Perhaps equally, we have visited a home that was cluttered and even smelled a bit like last night's dinner.

I would like to share regarding homes you have seen on "Real Wives of ... Wherever" and the antichrist version of the same.

I will preface with a particularly important point. Large financial resources or the extreme lack thereof have absolutely no bearing on whether a person has good taste and is equally neat and tidy. Nor does said dinero prevent them from being a complete slob with blinders permanently installed so as to never see the piles in the kitchen or a lack of olfactory senses that would make them oblivious to the fact that eight cats cannot share two cat boxes.

Please allow me to elaborate.

Query: What is the difference between rich and wealthy?
Rich people have money. Wealthy people have time.

Rich folks have the money to buy things they want, things that exist. That privilege can indeed go from one direction to another. Rich people may simply spend money on stuff and pile up that stuff. Wealthy people, on the other hand, have so much money that they have the time to dream up crap that should never exist.

Bear in mind, most of either of these two categories are relatively responsible with their finances and spend time, energy, and money being kind with family and generous in philanthropic fashions.

I am not picking on them. I am revealing the blackly comedic way money can be and often is spent on stuff you never knew could exist. Things that are perverse, pointless, stupid, inane and that truly evoke no response other than ... WTF?

I never cared much about those aspects. I usually think to myself, "Somebody made a killing on that," and I'm happy for the person that provided such a pointless item.

Back to the "judging by the cover" point of view.

You've seen those TV shows about celebrity homes. Well, we've been in them. While there are so many in the same realm of WTF, I do recall a particular favorite.

The work ticket today is a common problem. This report is about needing to properly connect the interior phone wiring after the generic telco techs, hired to save the rich person's contractor a few bucks, screwed the job up, and now the contractor will go way over that original budget hiring me to do the work correctly.

I drive down the entry road, at least a block long, towards the house recently built on a lake shore. Lots of beautiful stone and timber façade adorn two and three-story roof peaks. I did expect to find a service drive area yet found none and so parked right in front. I step up to the main door, and the bell rang out an impressive, deep, "Diiing-Dooong."

A long moment later, the door swings open, and there stands a delightfully endowed porn star in her morning yoga outfit.

"Uh ... Good Morning, I'm with the telephone company. My contact name is Ms. J. Public."

"I am she."

"Very good, ma'am" (Did I actually say, "Very good, ma'am"?).

"The trouble report indicates there are wiring issues. Would you be so kind as to elaborate and show me what and where the problems are?"

As the missus shows me about and explains problems, I begin to notice the beautiful layout and design of the structure. Then I start to take in the décor.

Plenty of obviously expensive ... schlock.

Items of art, furniture and assorted utilitarian items that individually must have cost a small fortune. Styles, colors, and design that only go together in a random church garage sale.

All I can surmise is that the Mr. or Mrs. convinced each other that they could indeed be their own interior designers (Oh, kinda like when they thought hiring a generic telephone wire company was a good call).

But what about the alternate universe of pretentious B.S.?

Trailer parks, mobile home communities, government subsidized housing, low-income, predominantly ethnic of whichever ethnicity, trailer-trash town, the 'hood, the barrio, little Asia, etc. All the accurate terms and the slang nicknames. You've heard them, and we've seen them.

The difference here is what we've seen in these hoods that most people never view past their bigoted blinders. That would be - pride.

More often than not, folks that live in these areas do so out of a purposeful need. They are working very hard on an education while keeping food on the table for the family. They are primary care people for an elderly parent. They recently took ill themselves and lost a job as a result.

Many have grown up in this 'hood and have a sense of community in their heart to stay and facilitate the needed changes of improvement even when city government, developers, and imposing industries are constantly threatening them and their homes.

I have been in these houses. I see this individual's personality. On more than one occasion, I've been in the barrio at some slumlord property. From the curbside, the property is obviously ignored by the landlord. However, on closer inspection, the yard and porch are quite tidy.

As the Madre greets me at the door, already apologizing for her broken English, I am aware of the delectable aroma of enchiladas. As she explains, "the phone not workeeng," I see that the house, while hardly decorated by the latest, trendy big-box decor store, is indeed, immaculate.

This dear lady works her ass off all day cooking and cleaning for the comfort of the children and the spouse who's working TWO jobs.

Bear in mind, while the landlord has no priority regarding this property, this darling woman treats the house as an absolute castle.

The moral of the story?

Keeping up with the Jones' might not be as good as taking a hint from the Jiménez's.

HOUSE ON MINNESOTA

I drive down the street of a mostly deserted neighborhood, scanning for the address on my service order. I notice three condemned houses on my left, the side of the street where my house is supposed to be, and I'm thinking, "They've gotten the wrong address on this house," because these are all abandoned ... or are they?

As I pull over, I see signs of someone living in the last house - the windows aren't boarded up, there's an old wooden screen door, and the front door is open. OK, no numbers on the house, but maybe this is it.

I get out and put my tool belt on, walk up to the door, and, before I can knock, an elderly woman is opening the screen door with a warm smile on her face, beckoning me inside.

"I'm here to install a phone line for you, ma'am."

"Yes," she says. "My children are worried about me living here, and they are paying for it. I don't think I need it, but they insist, so ... " Her voice trails off, and I am looking around her living room and beginning to realize there is no electricity in this house. No lamps, no television, no overhead lights on.

I ask her where she would like the jack installed, and she defers to my judgment, saying I know better. I suggest the bedroom - the phone would be right by her bed at night, and I can give her an extra-long cord, so she can take it in the living room, too.

She seems pleased by that answer, so I go into her bedroom and am looking around wondering how I'm going to drill the holes I need to run the wire. I'm looking at the floors, and I suddenly realize they are dirt floors, with area rugs placed throughout the small house.

Here's the thing: this house was immaculate. There was not a thing out of place; it was clean and obviously well taken care of. I was overwhelmed by this sense of respect and awe.

At that moment, I learned a lesson I have never forgotten: it's what a person has inside of them - self-respect and humility and willingness to make the best out of whatever their situation is - that determines how they live, what their lives look like. It has nothing to do with how much money or how many possessions you have or don't have.

I blinked back tears and told her I'd be right back. As I walked to my truck, I was desperate to find a way to get some power, so I could use my electric drill and do this job. I looked across the street and there were lights on in the house directly across from my customer's.

I walked over and knocked on their door, and a man answered. I explained what I was trying to do and asked if he would mind if I plugged my extension cords into one of his outlets and if he had any extension cords I could borrow because I knew I didn't have enough to go clear across the street.

He looked at me and smiled the biggest damn smile and said, "We'll get you some power all right." Between the two of us, we managed to cobble together enough cords to reach my customer's house.

So, it was a team effort, and, within an hour or so, this woman had a working phone line in her house.

I asked if there was anything else I could do, and she said, "Could I call my daughter and you can tell her what my new number is?"

We did exactly that, even had her daughter call her back so she knew the phone would ring okay.

Her daughter thanked me and told me she and her brothers weren't sure if having a phone line was possible since their mom didn't have electricity, that they had tried to convince her to move in with one of them, but she wouldn't hear of it. She was just fine where she was.

She was more than fine. This beautiful, proud woman didn't know it, but she made an indelible impression on this young technician. That was over thirty years ago, and I will never, ever forget her.

I'LL WAIT ON THE PORCH WHILE YOU GET DRESSED

There are probably any number of reasons a seemingly intelligent human being would answer the front door wearing only a bath towel. Here are some of those stories and, of course, the running narrative in my head when confronted by customers in various stages of dress. Or undress.

It was a Saturday morning, my first job that day. I was on the porch knocking at 8:30 a.m., and, after several minutes, the door was opened by a not very happy older woman, I'm guessing mid-sixties or so. She is wearing a t-shirt and clearly just got out of bed.

She says not a word but motions for me to come in. I am introducing myself when she turns around, and the back of the t-shirt is considerably shorter than the front, allowing me the unwelcome visage of her mid-sixties naked butt in what is clearly a losing battle with gravity.

I said to the back of her head, "I'll wait on the porch while you get dressed."

Seriously, why would you ever answer the door in a bath towel? Men and women both. Were you expecting someone else? I hope you were. I hope you and your lover had a tryst set up, and I just happened to show up first. Sorry!!

And what? You're going to just "hop in the shower real quick" and, "Go ahead and do what you need to do. I'll be out in a few minutes."

No, no, no. There's no showering while the telephone technician is at your house. It's a bad, bad idea. Not that I think you would ever, EVER, say that something inappropriate occurred while you were in the shower. Naked. While a complete stranger is in your home.

Here's the deal. Here's how this works: If you need to get in the shower, you can reschedule. I'll go ahead and leave, you can call the business office when you're done. Thanks! Rinse and repeat!

Ok, then there's the robe. Maybe pajamas underneath, maybe not. Let's just assume you ARE wearing pajamas. One young woman had me follow her into the kitchen as she explained what is going on with her phone while she was making some tea.

She turned on the gas burner, reached across the now lit burner to pick up the teapot, and her entire sleeve burst into flames! Whoosh! She was so stunned she just froze. I, however, went into freak-out mode and slammed her arm on the counter and started beating the fire out.

It took a few seconds but other than singeing the hair on her arm, she really wasn't hurt. I think she was a bit embarrassed, but all I was thinking was, "I just put out a fire on my customer." That's what I call Customer Service.

Let's talk about negligees. Let's talk about boxers vs briefs because we didn't have a long enough national conversation about that issue during the Clinton administration. Let's talk about seethrough, sexy underwear - there were times I was thinking, "Thank you baby Jesus, for what she's wearing right now" while simultaneously refusing to go in the house precisely because of what she is wearing right now.

I understand when a woman feels comfortable walking around in very little clothing in front of me because I'm a woman. It's just the lesbian factor that can throw me off a little sometimes.

Now, when a guy shows up at the door in his underwear, that is a different kind of wrong. Maybe it's just me (and all the straight guys I ever worked with), but nobody wants to see your junk. Unless you've hired an escort service you were expecting at 9 a.m., but otherwise, put your pants on. And if you have man breasts - for whatever reason, it doesn't matter - never under any circumstances go without wearing a shirt and maybe a training bra. Just sayin'.

So, you're probably wondering, "Did anyone answer the door completely naked?" Amazingly, no. But, there was the guy who left his front door unlocked with a note saying, "Phone company, please come in, I'm expecting you."

Well, I'll give him that. I yelled as I stuck my head in the door, "Ma Bell here!"

He yells back, "Come down the hall, first door on your left," and I follow his voice ... into the bathroom where he is in the bathtub, yep, completely naked and mostly submerged if you get my meaning ... like a little periscope breaking the surface of the water.

And not just a little under the influence of drugs and/or alcohol.

I backed out of the bathroom, down the hall, and out the door. I left a card on the front doorknob with the number to call to reschedule. Needless-to-say, that was the first and only time I entered a house based on a note taped to the front door.

There are countless examples of little kids answering the door completely naked. We'll chalk that up to not knowing better or watching mommy and daddy.

LOOK WHAT I GOT

I was down in the basement of this house, standing on a three-foot step-ladder with my hands shoved into a way-too-small space above the ceiling, trying to splice two wires together pretty much by touch alone. I had my small flashlight between my teeth, trying futilely to train it on the wiring.

What you may not know is after you hold a flashlight so long in your mouth, you start drooling. It must be the body's natural response. At least that's what I told myself.

Anyway, I was so focused on this task that I didn't hear the footsteps coming down the stairs, didn't notice anyone else being in the room with me until I heard the voice of a child say, quite proudly "This is my daddy's gun."

I stopped what I was doing and looked over to my left and there, holding what looked to be a shotgun or maybe a rifle, was a boy of about eight or nine years of age. He could barely hold the damn thing up, but he sure had it aimed at me. I remember having this exact thought:

"You are fucking kidding me that I'm going to die like this."

I held my hands up, stepped off the ladder, and said in the calmest voice I could muster, "Can you put that gun down please?"

He was smiling, pleased with himself (such a big boy!), but he did lower the barrel, so it was pointing at the floor.

I yelled up the stairs, "Ma'am, can you come down here? Please! I need you to come down here right now!"

I heard her footsteps cross the floor above me, and then she appeared in the doorway and made her way downstairs. The shock on her face matched the fear in my heart as she saw her son holding the gun. "Oh my God! Oh my God, I am so sorry!"

She took the gun and her child upstairs, muttering something about, "I told his father not to show him where he kept this."

After several long seconds, I was able to finish what I was doing, grateful to be alive and still in disbelief that I'd had a gun held on me by a nine-year-old. I never did ask if it was loaded.

OH, THE THINGS WE FIND

My service order said, 'customer requests jack in bathroom.' Yes, back in the days before cell phones or even cordless phones, we would install a jack pretty much anywhere.

Bathrooms had their own challenges, first and foremost, the fact that you're installing a jack with copper wiring in an extremely humid if not outright wet environment.

Often the customer had a medical condition or a disability that warranted them needing to be able to call for help from the bathroom, or maybe it was just the novelty of the idea.

This particular customer would certainly fall under the latter category, and that just may be an understatement.

The house was in a nice neighborhood, upper middle class, big homes. Not ostentatious like some areas but, definitely well-off. The lawn, the landscaping, and the pool, all well taken care of by professionals.

I rang the doorbell, and, when my customer opened the door and let me in, I observed and made judgments on two things: the interior of this house immediately made me think of a bordello and, secondly, it was clear no woman lived here.

Why do I say this? Well, there was an abundance of bad taste in both the furniture and the art (a term I use loosely) that was displayed on the walls. Also, the chair in the corner that looked like a giant pair of breasts.

My customer was one of those guys in his early fifties who is desperately fending off aging by dressing too young, wearing flashy jewelry, and a pre-Trump comb-over that I had a hard time not staring at when he wasn't looking.

Dark paneling and a sunken living room. Pretty sure there was red velvet on the loveseat, but it was hard to tell with the plastic covering it.

He tells me the bathroom where he wants the jack installed is upstairs, the private bath off the master bedroom.

"I have kind of an unusual bathroom," he says, chuckling, as I follow him up the stairs. I roll my eyes, thinking 'unusual' is a nice euphemism for tacky.

We walk into the bedroom, and there is the proverbial circular bed in the middle of the room, with an equally large circular mirror mounted on the ceiling over the bed. And, I shit you not, red shag carpeting.

My first instincts about the bordello décor are proving to be right, and I'm not exactly happy about that. I reach into my tool pouch, find the handle to my biggest flathead screwdriver just in case I have to stab my customer in self-defense and follow him into the master bath.

That's when it got really weird.

My customer steps into a large bathroom, with a double vanity and a shower roomy enough for four people. He tells me he wants the jack installed by the toilet, and that's when I see the snakes. Not live snakes, mind you, oh no.

These used to be live snakes, but now they are forever embalmed in the clear acrylic toilet seat. You know, so you can sit on a bunch of small, colorful, dead snakes in formaldehyde while you're relieving yourself. The toilet tank lid was exactly the same.

Now, several things are going through my mind as I'm taking this all in. In no particular order they are:

What. The. Fuck.

Why me?

What is it with the snakes?

Would my customer be offended if I gave him the number of a reputable interior decorator?

Has Elvis left the building, or did he just move to Kansas?

I know he is waiting for some reaction and I'll be damned if I'm going to give this necro-herpetologist the satisfaction. Yes, I made up the term, and it means 'dead snake collector.' It's sad that I had to invent a category for this weirdo.

"I am not drilling through your tile floor. It could shatter. What I'd like to do, instead of installing a floor jack, is run the line through this outside wall and around the side of the house. I'd recommend a wall phone in here. Far less chance of it getting wet."

"That's fine, that's fine. As long as you can get a jack in here. What do you think about the snakes?"

I take a breath. "Well, I can honestly say I've never seen a toilet like this before," and I am hoping this will be the end of it.

"I had this custom made. That's why!!" he tells me proudly.

What? They don't carry these at Home Depot?

These aren't full grown snakes either, so what happened there? You make a special purchase at the pet store of about twenty little baby snakes, so you can kill them somehow and then have somebody strategically place them inside a clear toilet seat?

I don't even want to know the thought process behind that.

"It is unique, I'll grant you that. I'm going to get my drill and a box of wire, and I'll be right back." And with that, I exit the Commode de Serpents, walk past the round bed (yes, I did wonder if it rotated and no, I did not ask), and go outside to the interface on the back of the house.

I disconnect the inside wiring, so my customer won't pick up the phone as I page one of my buddies on the crew. Within a minute or so he calls me.

"Hey, Grant, is there any chance you could swing by this job I'm on?"

Grant says sure, asks what's going on, and listens as I say the words 'circular bed,' 'mirror' and 'snakes in the toilet seat.'

"Oh, hell yes. I've got to see this. I'll be there in ten minutes," and he hangs up.

I breathe a sigh of relief as I walk back to my truck. This customer has not said or done anything inappropriate, but I've learned to trust my instincts with situations like this. Better safe than sorry.

Besides, sometimes you just have to share the weirdness.

TEMPTATION

It was summer, already hot that morning, and it was only ten o'clock. I rang the doorbell and waited. No one came. I rang it a second time and started to think no one was home when someone started turning the doorknob and struggling to open the door.

When it swung open, there was a kid standing there in a pair of Superman underwear. He was probably five years old.

I was just about to ask him if his parents were home when his mom appeared on the landing behind him. She was wearing a silky lace camisole that grazed the top of her thighs. I thought, "she must have been expecting a guy to come out," and then introduced myself.

She says she's glad to see women doing this kind of work. I smile and tell her I'm going to check the interface on the back of her house first to see if the trouble on her phone line is inside or outside the house.

This happened quite often, people answering their door in various stages of undress. It never ceased to surprise me, mostly because I couldn't fathom how anyone would think that was okay. Men and women, bath towels wrapped around them, or just a robe with nothing on underneath, different types of underwear or lack thereof.

My stock answer was either, "I'll wait out here while you get dressed," if I had to go inside, or tell them I needed to get in the backyard. You know, take a moment to get dressed since a total stranger is on your doorstep.

She says, "Okay. The gate's open. Help yourself."

I told her I'd let her know what I find, and I'm thinking surely she'll finish getting dressed while I'm back there.

There's a huge deck on the back of the house with steps leading down to the yard, and the interface is on the house, facing the bottom steps.

I've just opened the interface and am isolating the wire that is causing the trouble when I hear the sliding glass door open above me. She asks if I'd like some water, and I politely decline. But here she comes down those steps. I glance up, and she has not put anything on, still in that camisole.

I drop my eyes and continue working. She sits down on the steps so her legs are at my eye level and says, "Lord, isn't it hot out today?"

Without turning around, I agree that it is surely hot out today. A beat or two goes by and she says, "You look familiar. Have I seen you out at the Fantasy?"

This is one of the most popular gay bars in town, and one I frequent quite often. It is very possible she has seen me there. But I am wary of saying so to this woman, first because I'm at work and second because I'm thinking, "She has a kid. Is she married? What's going on here?"

So, I don't say anything. I turn to look at her, and, as I do, she slowly spreads her knees apart, and my eyes go where they shouldn't go just long enough to make me blush and make her smile as she watches me.

We lock eyes, and she tells me her husband is an over-the-road truck driver and is out of town right now.

Sweet Jesus on the turnpike ... in rapid succession, I think, "This is a trap. Her husband's inside the house with either a gun or a riding crop, and this is six ways to Sunday fucked up."

Now, because I am a little (or maybe more than a little) crazy I think, "What if he really is gone?"

Then a miracle happens, dressed in Superman underpants and flying down the deck steps to my rescue, excitedly talking about Oreo cookies for breakfast and some cartoon he was watching, her son appears. He sits down next to his Mama, and she pulls him close to her.

"Maybe you'll buy me a drink next time I see you out."

I look at her and tell her, "If I see you out I will absolutely buy you a drink."

God, I love this job.

SCOTT CITY

One of the advantages of having one phone company that served the entire United States was our ability to send technicians anywhere in the USA, and we could immediately do our job. The facilities, the central offices, and the way the phone company worked, in general, were the same everywhere.

This was especially important in service-emergencies where we might send techs in from several different states depending on the severity of the emergency. Give me a map, an actual fold-out roadmap, and I could work in any city in the country.

This was also true of special projects the phone company had going on in the state of Kansas. Post-divestiture, there was a project implemented in Kansas that was the result of an agreement between the Kansas Corporation Commission (KCC) and Ma Bell. This was a way to level the playing field for our consumers, our competitors, and for our company in the wake of divestiture.

For the history of its existence, the cost of local telephone service was subsidized by long distance, allowing Ma Bell to offer local service at extremely reasonable rates. It was a pretty simple business equation: long distance calling was conducted over an existing system of Ma Bell wires and required very little maintenance and so was profitable.

What was not profitable was the initial installation and the recurring maintenance of urban and especially rural landlines. Ma Bell, up to that point, had to provide service to anyone who wanted a phone.

Say Joe Customer wanted a phone line in his new house that was ten miles away from his closest neighbor; Ma Bell absorbed the cost of providing that customer with phone service. It may cost Ma Bell tens of thousands of dollars to lay ten miles of cable to this customer's house, and we did so with no additional charge.

If the same Joe Customer decided in six months that he wanted to use one of our competitors instead of us for local service, that competitor would use Ma Bell facilities to provide their service.

With very few exceptions, anytime a consumer uses one of our competitors, that dial tone is being delivered on Ma Bell facilities and maintained by Ma Bell technicians. There are very few companies that have actually built their own networks at their expense.

My point in telling you all of this is that in order for there to be parity between Ma Bell and our competition, we agreed to some conditions set down by the KCC. Competitors wanted to be able to offer services only Ma Bell had been capable of providing up to that point, like long distance and local service. Ma Bell, on the other hand, wanted to compete with the television/cable companies.

To be able to do this, Ma Bell and KCC agreed that party lines would be phased out, and everyone who had a phone line from Ma Bell would have their own private line. No more sharing one line with between two and eight people, listening for the specific ring that told you the call was for you and not your neighbor two miles down the road.

Part of the reasoning behind this was a new technology coming out called broadband, which required a dedicated, private line in order to work. This would allow consumers to have access to high-speed internet in their homes. It would, as you already know, revolutionize the world of telecommunications.

Which brings me to Scott City.

Two factors came into play in my being sent out to Scott City, Kansas. First, I was one of only three female installer/repair technicians in the area at that time. Second, my uncle was the second-line manager, and he told me he wanted to send a female tech and that I was going. End of story.

Another tech and I were being sent, and there were about a half-dozen technicians from other areas in Kansas that were going as well.

The citizens of Scott City didn't know it yet, but they were all getting private lines over the next several weeks. At the time, about half of the townspeople and everyone who lived outside of town had party lines.

To demonstrate what kind of task this was, think about this: Where eight people had once been served by one single pair of copper wires for however many miles they lived from the central office, now those same eight people were to be served by eight separate pairs of copper wires dedicated to each of their homes.

It was a huge undertaking that required new cable to be buried and telephones to be completely rewired or exchanged. But more than anything it required us, the technicians on the front lines, to explain what all the fuss was about.

There were many people who were just fine with using a party line, thank you very much. They didn't understand why the phone company needed to do this at all. They didn't even own a computer, so why did they have to have a private line if they didn't want broadband? It was up to us to explain how this was, ultimately, a good thing, and that it was required by the state of Kansas.

Aside from customer wariness, Scott City was a bit of culture shock for me. Everyone knew each other, and the guy who worked in the Ma Bell central office was also chief of the volunteer fire department and, of course, the mayor as well. Which made it really easy to reach him because if he wasn't in the central office, you could call the diner or city hall or his house and, by God, he could be back at the central office in three minutes from any of those other locations on foot.

There was also a huge Mennonite population of farm families who lived outside of Scott City. I swear they all had the same last name. I would pull up to a farmhouse with Unruh on the mailbox and half the time whoever answered the door would say, "That's not me," and go on to tell me the particular Unruh I was looking for was their second cousin on their Mama's side, and, to get to their house, I needed to go on down the road two miles and turn right at the driveway with the mailbox mounted on an old plowshare and... well, you get the idea.

I remember one house where I was refused entry. The woman who answered the door was wearing an ankle length Calico dress and a matching bonnet, and her hair was pulled back so severely it looked like it was painful. I could see her garments were all homemade.

She looked me up and down. I don't think she could have been any more surprised if I'd just landed in her yard in a spaceship. Her eyes darted from me to my truck, taking in my blue jeans and the tool belt on my hips. In a few seconds, I saw confusion and apprehension and maybe disgust play across this woman's face.

"What do you want?" she asked sharply.

"I'm here to convert your party line into a private line, ma'am. Do you remember getting a notice in the mail about that? I'll need to rewire all your phones in the house." At that, she cuts me off.

"You can't come in. The phone company needs to send a man out."

I am taken aback by this and I say, "It won't take me but a few minutes to rewire your sets. It would be another four or five days to get one of the guys out here."

"You are not coming in this house. Please have them send a man out. I need to ask you to leave our property." She is clearly uncomfortable, and I see there is no way she will allow me to perform the work.

"Alright, ma'am. I'll let the local supervisor know about your request. You'll need to call the business office and let them know when you'll be available. I'll be on my way."

I hand her a card with my name and the local numbers to the Ma Bell offices. She accepts the card and closes the door without another word to me.

I step off the porch and walk back to my truck parked in the dirt road at the foot of the drive, put my tool belt away, and am sitting in my cab doing paperwork. Out of the corner of my eye, I see someone come around the corner of the house, walking quickly towards me.

It's a young girl, maybe fifteen or sixteen, wearing a similarly long dress and bonnet, only it's even stranger seeing such conservative garb on a teenager. She looks back towards the house a couple of times as she approaches, and I get the sense that the woman who answered the door would not approve of what this young girl is doing. Then I wonder if Mennonites believe in owning guns. Or maybe crossbows. I tell myself to rein it in as the girl steps up to my window.

"Hi! Where are you from?" she asks me excitedly.

"I'm from Wichita, Kansas. My name is Shelley." I smile at this kid, and she tells me her name is Gwen, short for Gwendolyn, and then she bombards me with questions.

"How big is Wichita? Do you like your job? What music do you listen to? How many high schools are in Wichita? How long have women worked in jobs like this? What movies are showing where you live? How much does a pair of jeans cost?"

I answer all of her questions, and it occurs to me it's as if Gwen just stepped out of a time capsule. In a way, she has. I ask her what grade she is in, and her answer shocks me.

"I don't go to school anymore." I assume she graduated, and when I say so she corrects me.

"No, I didn't graduate. I would be a junior this year. I'm promised to someone now. Our parents arranged it. I'll work on our farm until we get married, and then I'll move to his family's farm."

I wonder how she feels about this and am about to ask when the front door flies open and her mother is striding towards us. I'm pretty sure she could conceal a crossbow in the folds of her dress.

"Thank you for talking to me!" Gwen has a wistful look on her face, and part of me wants to kidnap this kid and bring her into the twentieth century. Her entire life has been decided for her, and I can't even begin to comprehend living like that.

I tell her how much I enjoyed meeting her and start my truck up. She is walking backwards and waving to me as I pull away. I wish her good luck, and, as I drive back into town, I reflect on the stark contrast between our very different lives.

It is a small comfort knowing that the technology we are bringing can provide these young people with information and with that, choices and options that, until now, they didn't even know they had.

Not everyone was happy to get their own private line. There was some skepticism as to why this had to be done, and change isn't easy for a lot of people.

I had been out to this elderly lady's house about three days earlier and changed her over to a private line. She understood when I explained to her why everyone was required to have a private line, but she didn't like it. She had two sets that I rewired and everything was in good working order when I left her house that day.

Now I have a trouble report in my hands for her address. The report says: phone line not working since technician left. No tech wants to see a report like that. I'm glad the ticket didn't go to another technician because I want to see what is going on with her phone line.

She remembers me when she answers her door and greets me warmly. I ask her what kind of trouble she's been having since I left. She is shaking her head as she motions me to follow her into the kitchen.

She has a rotary wall phone that has to be thirty years old. It has one of those twenty-five-foot cords on the handset that now reaches over thirty feet because it's been stretched so much. It took me five minutes last time I was out to just untangle the damn thing. She picks up the handset, gives it to me and says, "Just listen to that."

I dial the local time and weather number, so I can listen to her line while a call is made. I don't hear anything—no static, no hum on the line. Of course, I tested the line before I came out and didn't see any trouble then, but I tell her I'll be back, and I hook up my test set at the interface and run another test.

No trouble detected on the line. I go back inside and tell my customer that I am not finding anything wrong with her line. She picks up the handset, dials the weather line herself and after a few seconds she says, "It's doing it right now," and hands me the phone. I listen to it intently but again, I don't hear anything.

"Ma'am, I have to tell you I don't hear anything on this line at all."

Her face breaks into a grin and she says, "That's what I mean! It sounds dead!"

It takes a couple of beats before I realize that the private line is so quiet compared to the party line she'd been on for her entire life that she thought it wasn't working properly.

"This is what a private line sounds like, ma'am. It should be quiet." She is skeptical as I replace the handset in the cradle.

"Well, it just doesn't seem right. I guess I called you out here for nothing," she says apologetically.

I smile and assure her that this change over to private lines has been an adjustment for most everyone out here and to let us know if she has any more questions.

As I drive away from her house, I smile and shake my head. A trouble ticket saying the line is too quiet? I'll take one of those reports any time.

Scott City was a good experience for me not only for the kind of work I was doing and the money I made while I was there, but it gave me some exposure to the small-town way of life. Things like walking into the only bar in town with a couple of my coworkers looking for a place to have a drink after a hard day's work.

There was a bartender behind the bar and a table full of old men playing dominoes. Everyone turned to look at us when we walked in, and, just as quickly, went back to the dominoes game. We had some watered-down beer on tap and from that night on we stayed in our motel rooms to drink whiskey and beer we picked up at the local liquor store.

One of my coworkers from another small town in Kansas made a bong from a lead cable sleeve. He'd hammered it and soldered it and it looked like it might actually work. It must have weighed ten pounds, and while we all admired it for the craftsmanship, we did point out that no one should smoke anything from a lead bong. It could, however, be used as a weapon.

One of my buddies I'd been sent out there with, Brodie, decided we should mess with the motel staff a little bit. We both got wake-up calls from the front desk every morning, so Brodie got up early and came down to my room in time for my wake-up call.

He answered the phone when the front desk called my room, and all I heard was his side of the conversation. It was enough.

"Good morning." Long pause.

"No, no mistake. This is Shelley's room." Long pause.

"This is her wake-up call? I'll wake her up, sure. She's right here".

At this point, Brodie is trying so hard not to laugh that he has to cover up the mouthpiece of the phone. I sit on the bed, shaking my head and wondering how this is going to come back on me.

"Hey, she's awake now! Do you want to speak to her? No? Ok, well thank you for calling! Bye, now."

He hangs up and is thoroughly satisfied with himself. We decided to wait ten minutes and then the two of us walk through the lobby on our way to our phone trucks. I can only describe the looks I got from the two older women behind the front desk as 'Die, Tramp' and 'Repent, Ye Sinner.'

I make up my mind to talk to both of them before we leave town, letting them in on the joke. I'm starting to think about the explaining

I'd have to do if this got back to our supervisors. Time for a little damage control.

I was in Scott City for almost four weeks, though it seemed a lot longer. I learned a lot in that time, like the fact that out in western Kansas, the tarantulas are so big you can actually see them moving through the grass from up on a pole.

Brodie caught one and put it in a glass jar he got somewhere, poking holes in the lid like we did in grade school. I didn't even know there were tarantulas in Kansas, and I sure didn't know they were as big as a person's hand. They are beautiful in their own way, preferably from a distance.

I gained confidence and learned that I could go anywhere the company sent me to work. I gained an appreciation for the slow pace of a small town, but I couldn't wait to get back home just to hear some music that wasn't country.

More than anything, I came away grateful for the choices and opportunities I had as a young woman.

THE BAD AND NOT SO GOOD STUFF

Walking into someone's home, you never know what or who you might encounter. Sometimes you wish you could unsee what you just saw.

Case in point:

I was on a repair ticket; the report was that the customer was having trouble connecting to the internet. When I arrive at the apartment, a woman answers the door and tells me the phone line is downstairs, and she'll show me where the computer is.

She leads me to the basement door, and it's locked, which I think is a bit odd, but as she finds the key in her pocket she explains.

"He lives down here. I don't come down here too often, but he's at work, so he gave me his key to let you in."

The basement looks like a guy lives here. Clothes strewn about, dirty dishes piled up, ashtrays overflowing with cigarette butts. A sour odor permeates the room; just being down here is depressing.

I ask how old this guy is; she replies that he is thirty-two. Staying here temporarily, lost his good job a couple of months ago, trying to get back on his feet. She is sitting at his desk, turning the computer on.

"I guess you'll want to see what happens when he tries to go online."

I say, "No, I can check our signal with my equipment, so I don't really need you to turn that on."

But it is on, and she is moving the mouse around and clicks on a folder on the desktop. It opens up and immediately there must be fifty thumbnails filling the screen. Each one is titled, and I am reading words like:

'Five-yr. old boy chained'

'12-yr. old girls with multiple men'

'Fully nude 3-yrs old'

The reality of what I am seeing hits me in the stomach, and I am at once sickened and outraged.

The woman doesn't seem to be paying attention. She is saying, "This isn't what I'm looking for. Where is it?" and clicks out of that folder.

I look at the screen, and there are many other folders filling the desktop. I tell her quietly to go ahead and shut the computer down. I'd seen enough.

I don't think that she is aware of what she has just shown me. I tell her I need to check the interface on the back of the house, then I go to my truck to get my test equipment.

Once I have my equipment hooked up to the line, I kneel down and lean my forehead against the side of the house. I am so disturbed by the child pornography on this man's computer that I feel like I might throw up. I pray he doesn't come home while I'm here because I'm not sure how I would respond. I have to do something, but I'm not sure how to handle this. I take a few deep breaths and

154

think, "Just get this job done first and get out of here. Then I'll figure it out."

All the rest of that day I go back and forth. Should I tell my supervisor? Go to my Union rep? Tell one of my coworkers I trust? Finally, I look up the local Bureau of Investigation number. I've decided I'm going to do this anonymously if I can, without bringing anyone else at the company into it.

"I need to report some child pornography I saw today on a customer's computer. I work for Ma Bell, and I don't want the customer to know who reported him. I don't want to jeopardize my job."

The agent I spoke with assured me my name would be kept confidential. I gave him all the information I had on this guy – address, phone number, how long his phone number had been in use, his social security number, his age, that he is living in the basement of someone's apartment. That I didn't believe this person was aware of what she had inadvertently opened-up on the computer.

He asked me a few more questions and told me I was doing the right thing. I asked if the agency would tap his line.

"I can't tell you specifically what will happen, but I will tell you we are going to follow up on your report. We do have a couple of operations that are ongoing, and the first thing we'll do is see if this guy is already on our radar."

OK. It was done. I felt greatly relieved when I hung up the phone, and I had no doubt I'd done the right thing. As I reflected back on what happened, I thought, maybe I was supposed to see that today. Maybe that all happened exactly so the investigative agency would be notified. Maybe, in some small way, this will help the children in those folders.

I'll never know but I hope so.

WORKING IN CUSTOMERS' HOMES

Going into customers' homes, we were on their turf, and that made for some interesting dynamics. People were generally trusting, especially when a Ma Bell truck was parked in front of their house and someone in a tool belt was at their door. I was rarely asked for any kind of identification, and I think that speaks to the good reputation Ma Bell had.

That same reputation sometimes worked against us. I was proud and grateful to be working for such a trusted company but no, you cannot leave your twelve-year-old here while you go to work. I can't count how many times there wouldn't even be an adult home, just a minor child to answer the door and tell the phone company what needed to be done. Or to hand me a note written by their parents.

Of course, we would never enter a home unless there was an adult present. I was just astonished that anyone would leave their kid at home to deal with a contractor/service person.

Occasionally I'd find a note on the front door:

Phone man, I had to leave before you got here, but the house is unlocked so you can come in and do your work. Here's my work number if you need to call about anything.

That's when I would hang one of our 'No Access' cards on the door handle with a short note explaining that AN ADULT needed to be present for us to perform the work. I refrained from saying that leaving a note taped to the front door that states your house is unlocked is just plain stupid.

Sometimes on our service orders or repair tickets, we'd be asked to call the customer at work before heading out, so they could meet us. Invariably the customer would say, "I'm ten minutes away."

No, they weren't. Just tell me how long it's really going to take you because if I'm still sitting in my truck thirty minutes after we spoke, and you haven't arrived, at 31 minutes I am hanging the 'No Access' card.

Half an hour later, the business office would page me wanting to know why I left before the customer arrived and could I go back. No, I can't because now I am working at the house of a customer who ACTUALLY SHOWED UP WHEN THEY SAID THEY WOULD.

I once had a customer leave while I was up on the pole! She left a note taped to my box of wire: *I was called into work unexpectedly. Please lock the door when you're done.*

Oh my God, I couldn't get hold of my supervisor fast enough! He told me to pack up my stuff and leave a note for the customer to call him directly. It was an awful position to be in as far as liability goes. No technician ever wants to be accused of stealing or damaging the customer's property. Fortunately, that didn't happen in this particular circumstance.

Of course, there were times when property did get damaged, and Ma Bell would certainly take care of that for our customers.

Then there were a few customers who saw an opportunity to benefit financially from these situations.

For example, I was drilling a hole to run a new wire, and, when I stood up, I accidentally knocked a mirror off the wall, breaking it in several pieces. I immediately told the customer, apologized and gave her both my supervisor's number and the claims department number. I also called my supervisor to let him know what happened.

I finished my work, and, before I even got to my next job, I got a page from my supervisor.

"That mirror you knocked off the wall. How much do you think it cost?"

"I don't know, maybe fifteen or twenty dollars. I mean, the backing on it was cardboard. Why?"

I hear him chuckling. "Your customer is saying it's an antique and it has sentimental value because it's an heirloom from her grandmother. So, you're saying it's not an antique?"

"No, hell no it's not an antique." I am rolling my eyes. Just for fun, I ask him how much the customer claimed the mirror was worth.

"Five hundred dollars."

"Ha! That's crazy talk! Are you going to see her? Have her show you the pieces. You'll see right away what I'm talking about."

"I am heading out there in about fifteen minutes. I have no doubt you're right, and I'll offer her a fair price for it. It'll never go to claims."

Turns out the customer was willing to take fifty dollars for that heirloom.

One of my favorite stories didn't happen to me but to one of my crewmates. Doug was installing a jack in an attic that had been converted into an office. He drilled a hole through the interior wall into the attic space and ran his wire through the hole, through the attic and outside to the interface. He had completed the job and was in his truck doing some paperwork when the customer came running outside.

"Mister! Mister! There's smoke coming out of the hole you drilled in my office!"

I think I can safely speak for all technicians when I say that is a sentence you never, ever want to hear come out of a customer's mouth.

Doug ran back into the house and up the stairs to the office. Sure as hell, just as the customer said, there was smoke trailing out of the hole the wire was run through.

At that moment, Doug knew what had happened. He had used a dull drill bit and it took longer to get through the wood stud, causing more friction which caused the drill bit to heat up which set the paper on the insulation between the walls on fire.

Doug made two calls in quick succession. The first was to 911 to report the fire, and the second was to his supervisor to tell him there was going to be a damage claim.

The supervisor didn't ask any questions, just told Doug he was on his way to the site. By the time he arrived there were two fire trucks at the premise. The supervisor frantically found Doug and asked if he was okay if he was hurt in any way.

"I'm okay," Doug assured him. "I almost set the guy's house on fire! Can you believe that?"

When he told me this story, Doug said his supervisor looked like his head might explode. That's when he looked at Doug and said, "If this ever happens again, would you mind mentioning that the fire department is here BEFORE I GET TO THE HOUSE?"

YOUR PHONE IS DOING WHAT?

When someone had trouble with their phone, they would call the repair department at Ma Bell and talk with a real live person who was in an office building in the SAME CITY AS THE CUSTOMER! What a concept! The customer would be asked what the trouble was, and there were some funny descriptions.

Or sometimes we'd show up, and the customer had diagnosed the trouble, knew exactly what we needed to do to fix it, and sometimes wanted to argue with us when the real trouble was not where the customer thought it was.

My trouble ticket said, 'Phone goes dead every time customer sits on couch.' No trouble was detected on the line at the time it was tested. When it was what we called 'come and go trouble,' or intermittent, the challenge was to catch it when it's causing the trouble or to be able to replicate it while we're there. When I arrived at my customer's house, he offered to demonstrate what happens.

"Okay." He is picking up the phone on the table by the couch. "Dial tone." He hands it to me, and I verify. He hangs it up, sits on the couch. I pick up the phone, and I have a dial tone.

"It's still working."

"No, no, no. Wait," and he scoots over to the end closest to the phone and the dial tone disappears. I push down on the switch hook, let it up – NO dial tone.

I smile as he grins in triumph and says, "I told you! The lady who took my report was laughing, but I told her I wasn't kidding!"

"I believe you. Stay right there. I want to check something while it's not working." With that, I step over to the jack the phone is wired into and kneel down on the carpet. I open the jack and see a non-standard wire hooked up to our wiring.

A couple of things: non-standard wiring was braided wire (several strands of copper filament twisted together) that was flimsy and was damaged easily. We didn't use it, but, since divestiture, customers could run their own wiring or hire someone else besides Ma Bell to do it. That's what I was looking at. Wiring someone had installed on their own.

I disconnected it from the jack, picked up the phone, and my dial tone is working. I hook up my test meter to the non-standard wire and there it is, a short. That short is causing the trouble. But what is causing the short?

I tell my customer to go ahead and get off the couch. He stands up and my short disappears. I have him sit down again and bang, my needle slams all the way over to the right. A solid short.

I pull on the non-standard wire, and, instead of being attached to the baseboard like the phone company would run a wire, it is running underneath the carpet and across the room. But before it gets completely across the room, it is firmly pinned underneath one of the thick legs of the couch where it has finally been damaged to the point that every time someone sits on the couch, the weight crushes the wiring together and the phone goes dead. Hence the very accurate trouble description given by this customer.

I tell the customer it is Ma Bell policy that we won't repair or replace any non-standard wiring, so it's up to him to decide what to do with the damaged wire. The good news is that now the customer can sit on his couch and still have a working phone.

SEPTEMBER 11, 2001

I remember one of the guys on my crew was sitting in his truck when he motioned me over. We were all out in the parking lot getting ready to head out that morning. He turned down the radio when I came up to the window.

"A plane just flew into the World Trade Center," he said.

It was a little after 8 a.m., and the world was just beginning to realize what was happening on this fateful morning. As he and I talked for several minutes, we thought the same thing that many people would think in those first awful moments - that it was an accident, the pilot was inexperienced, it was a small plane. A fluke.

I turned my radio on as I drove to my first customer's house. There wasn't any more information yet, not really.

When I arrived, my customer answered the door and immediately asked me if I'd heard what happened in New York. I told him I had, and he said he was watching on the news if I wanted to see. I said thanks and that I'd check once I got the work done.

He showed me where he wanted the jack installed, then he went back into his home office. I worked methodically, my mind going back to the news as I ran the wire around the outside of the house. I finished up and went downstairs to tell my customer I was done. He was in his office with the television on when I walked in.

Without looking at me he said, "The south tower is collapsing." His voice sounded so strange, incredulous, scared.

I remember thinking, "This can't be real," even as I watched the sickening affirmation of his words on the screen as the tower fell. We watched in silence together. I can't remember his name, but here we were, two strangers, watching this incomprehensible tragedy.

The loss of human life and the dawning realization that this was not an accident. I don't know how long we watched. At some point, I said I was leaving, and he told me to be safe.

Time seemed to stop. The world seemed to stop. I called my mom and my sister. I told them I loved them. I had a couple of customers cancel that day. The ones who were home or at their businesses were in the same state of shock that I felt. We all realized that nothing else was that important or mattered at this moment.

I can remember going on a couple of work orders, but most of that day is surreal when I think about it. It was so quiet, even the traffic just seemed to stop.

Of course, as the day went on, we would see that this was no accident. As the second and then the third plane crashed, we saw that it was intentional. We called it an 'act of terrorism,' and what had been going on in Europe, the Middle East, South Africa, and too many other nations had come to our shores in the United States.

Now, all these years later, there are many questions unanswered; many theories abound as to what really happened, who was responsible. I'm not going to go into my opinions around 9/11 and the subsequent actions taken by the Bush administration. This is not the place for that.

What I do know is that day changed the world. Much as the first Great War, World War II, Vietnam, and too many wars in between and since have altered history, so has 9/11.

As a telephone technician who had access into mechanical and electrical/telecommunication equipment rooms all over the city, I enjoyed the trust and confidence of my customers. As telephone techs, we were given keys/access to areas that other people would never be granted access to. No more.

We were no longer given the latitude we once had. Keys weren't checked out to us, knowing they'd be returned. It didn't matter how long we'd been working with a particular customer or business. It wasn't just certain offices or buildings; it was everywhere. It was everyone. Our collective trust had been broken.

People were scared and angry. Nothing would be the same. We would grudgingly accept that 'business as usual' was a thing of the past.

One thing has always struck me about that day: how many people called someone they loved and told them that they loved them - the souls in the World Trade Center, perhaps realizing their fate, the passengers on Flight 93, those of us watching as the horror unfolded before our eyes.

To me, those calls - the act of expressing love for someone in the face of such tragedy - those calls are what is best about human beings. That, in the midst of violence and death, our thoughts turn to the love in our hearts and we speak it out loud. We make sure our loved ones know it ... even if it is the last thing they hear us say. Especially if it is the last thing we ever say.

A UNIQUE AND COMPLETELY UNEXPECTED HISTORY OF THE TELEPHONE, THE TELEPHONE COMPANY, AND A FEW OTHER THINGS YOU DIDN'T THINK YOU NEEDED TO KNOW (BUT NOW YOU DO)

History basics of (mostly) American Telephony.

T ... phony ... What? Telephony is the actual term for the category of the type of business the phone company is. (For those of you who are already lost, please to refer to the glossary.)

Ready to start again? Good.

Essentially, it all began in the 17th century, 1667 to be exact. A guy named Robert Hooke invented *communications barnyard engineering* when he took a string, pulled it real tight, and came up with the first *two-cans-and-a-string* telephone.

About a hundred years later, Johann Reis, the son of a baker from Germany, got the tech rolling with his *Reis Telephone,* which electrically and clearly shot the human voice across a distance of, three-hundred feet!

Soon after Reis, a couple of cats by the names of Innocenzo Manzetti and Antonio Meucci, both Italian inventors working on and with telephone types of equipment, began the two-decade-long argument over who invented what and when regarding the beginnings of what we now know as the telephone. Wait ... were these guys ... gasp ... "Imergrints"?

While all this is transpiring, Elisha Gray figures the way to cash in will be to make stuff for this telephone thing, so he founded the Western Electric Manufacturing Co. in 1872.

Thomas Edison plays around with these toys a bit but loses interest and drops the subject.

Gray keeps thinking of ways to make money, while Alexander Graham Bell has a vision quest during a vacation in 1874.

About this same time, Edison has another great idea, but, once again, he blows it off.

Gray, Bell, and their respective lawyers battle out in the patent office until Bell wins on March 7, 1876, with the U.S. Patent, No. 174,465.

BTW ... It was not until 2002 that the U.S. House formally recognized Antonio Meucci for his work "IN the invention of" but not "FOR the invention of" the telephone. The same year, the Canadian Parliament unanimously declared Alexander G. Bell as the inventor of the telephone.

While all this American biz was transpiring, the very first commercial telephone company was open for business in Friedrichsberg, Germany. That company used equipment developed by the Siemens Co. Sound familiar?

A company startup called Western Union decides to try and keep Edison focused and busy. His development of the carbon-microphone transmitter sends and receives a call over a distance of one hundred and thirty miles.

Woohoo!

In this same time frame of 1878-ish, the first American telephone exchange (glossary time) begins and another exchange in London, as well one in Australia, opens-up.

Yeah, it's becoming a thing.

All the while, Edison, Bell, Francis Blake, and more inventors are making this, investors buying that, founders and owners arguing, and lawyers are finding a whole new world of cash to grab onto.

Around the mid to late 1880's, the first national telephone networks were established as well as services called pay-phones.

Fast forward to the dawn of Twentieth Century.

By the turn of the 19th – 20th centuries, the entity nicknamed Ma Bell began price wars as well as buying up other "independent" telcos.

In 1899, American Telephone and Telegraph buys its own subsidiary, American Bell Telephone Co. Why would someone do that? Well, to avoid government interference, of course, you see? The battle over the crap we deal with today started over one-hundred years ago.

The next fifty years of activities ranged from long distance network building, equipment design and development, which included wacky stuff like the study of over four-thousand people's skull sizes, to figure the best average distance from your ear to your lips in-order to decide the length and width of the old-school telephone receiver your grandmother had on the set next to her favorite chair.

Cables went into the oceans to connect main-lands to isle-lands. A video-phone call was made by President Herbert Hoover. (And you thought that shit was "new.")

The first around-the-world call was interconnected with wire and radio combined. Hell, the first mobile-phone call was made in 1946.

Jumping to just after World War Two, Microwave radio becomes the technology of choice for long distance calls. (It's not just for making popcorn and burritos.)

Modems, specifically their predecessors, were introduced for the use of teleprinters and telegraphs for the military and other government uses. Ever wonder why so many people refer to the internet as an aspect of Big Brother?

It was invented by Big Brother, duh.

Anyway ...

In the 1950's, Bell Labs introduced the small wonder known as the transistor. Oh, boy! More new toys.

Leaping into the future, the 1960's is where cell phones came from as well as touch-tone telephones and geosynchronous satellites (Telstar). These were the real days of R&D for the future yet to come.

During all this techie stuff, cool stuff like equal rights (ya know, for humans), and stupid stuff like wars and political corruption, were raging on as usual.

The 70's and the 80's continued developments regarding the tech born of the 50's and 60's to make practical and dependable electronic systems. These included electronic and digital switching systems for telco "Operator Services" (the "Zero" on the phone which also stood for the *letter* "O"), business and private telephone-switch multi-line equipment.

Included in these same types of research were aspects of the public version of the internet as well as ongoing improvements on cell-phone tower networks.

Caller-ID was developed from the research on digital *packets*, "Voice Over Internet Protocol (VOIP)" for all you coding geeks.

A fiber-optic cable was strung across the Atlantic about the same time The Gap Band and Duran Duran were touring. Oh, and in 1983, the LAST manual operator cord-board switchboard in the US (in

Maine) was finally retired.

By now, large corporations began to figure out that women and men could now do each other's jobs (???!).

Oh, and they found out that black guys are smart too (Who knew?). Spanish speaking people are capable of speaking more languages than most people in the US (oh, that can't be right) and capable of doing something besides making tacos or driveways (now you're just making stuff up). Indigenous tribes no longer chop down the telegraph poles (hey, but Grandpa said ...).

People from other countries are indeed like us (whatever 'us' is) ... just from another country.

What is the point? All these folks (humans) can and do comprise the history of the telcos.

Now ... the Dark Ages (as if all that other shit was not bad enough).

1984. Divestiture.

Hard to say if it was a good or bad year. Or both.

Uncle Sam told Ma Bell to kick all the freeloading children out of the house. "Go fend for yourselves, my children," says Ma.

So, for the next many years, trying to make all the "Baby Bells" be self-supporting adults put a bit of a damper on money previously used for product development.

Affordable cell phones and that internet thing were gonna-hafta wait just a bit. Well, Asymmetric Digital Subscriber Lines (ADSL) were introduced in 1987. Really fast digital circuits. Cool! That was something, anyway. Now, what to do with it?

By the 1990's, things like dial-up modems, pager systems, and cell-tower tech are trying to ramp-up.

In Finland, the first GSM (Global System of Communications) is launched with its first call. John and Jane Q. Public can now afford a cell phone. Rap is now mainstream music and Grunge is rebirthing rock and roll. (Yes, these points are relevant.)

Next on the timeline, beware, the "Boogie-Man" ... Y2K.

OK ... we did not blow up. Whole cities were not swallowed by Hades. Entire church choirs were not sucked into the sky. Extraterrestrials have still not fixed our political or world war issues.

Telecommunications are pretty much plodding along the path of research and development of better and faster circuits for the internet and cleaner, stronger signals for cell phone usage.

What became known as "File sharing" of the aforementioned music, indeed, was relevant in that the customers demanded faster circuits for this novelty called the "Internet" (it's just a fad and will fade out soon enough, eh?).

So, here we are in the present. The cusp of the end of landlines ... cough-bullshit ... It may not be made from copper, but fiber optic is still a ... landline.

The days of gravy-skimmers in the long-distance game or the inventing gadgets to make your touch-tone phone do something besides make a call are over.

The competition is now in the realm of cellular device tech and whatever some coder can dream up to fuck with the poor innocent internet user.

I cannot go too far into the subject of *end-user* equipment. Equipment is built for and by the private sector, and that is a different realm beyond the overall point of this book, and a rabbit hole we'll only peer into as you read.

I hope you've been enjoying.

GLOSSARY

This is the funniest glossary you'll never want to read (but you really should).

20-Foot Fence Post
Slang term for skinny utility pole.

Additional Line ("Add-Line")
Term for the second and even third landline in residential homes. Very popular about the time of puberty or mid-life crisis adultery.

Aerial
Adverb term for working aloft. Adjective for types of cable, or terminal. Not a popular cartoon character.

Belt
Body-belt. Parts of body-belt. Not whiskey or Tequila (yet).

Buried
Anything that we buried in the ground, drops, cables, splices,

electrocuted squirrels, your missing cat, or whatever.

Bond

No, not James, nor the connection you were certain you made with the bartender. In telco terms, this is the continuous set of connections to and of, a ground wire, ground rods, straps, strands, and other types of metallic objects that are connected securely to form a solid contact with Mother Earth.

Cable

Term used for the metallic paired wire, fiber optic, or coaxial gathering enclosure that is either buried in the ground, placed in underground raceways, or suspended in the air by way of a suspension strand and then mounted to utility poles. Cables appear similar to rope and extend for several feet to several miles. Also used as a communication medium to display the shoes of a dearly departed rival gang member.
Or:
Abbreviated term to describe a crew of technicians or a single technician whose single or primary functions are to install and or maintain the aforementioned wire, fiber, or coax cables.

Cat 5 (3, 2, etc.)

Abbreviated term for a type of "twisted pair" wire. Category (cat) 5, for instance, is a twisted pair that twists around itself five times in a linear inch (the number indicates the twist amount).
Note* The twist is a method that dissipates electromagnetic interference. The twist motion of the signal as it travels along the wire basically "shakes water (the electromagnetic interference) off the

duck's back".

Central Office

Where da dial tone comes from. Try making the NNNNNNNNNNNNNNNNNNNNNNNNNNNN sound (like your vibrator).

Conductor

A metallic wire or cable used to "conduct" the flow of electrical power and broadband signals. Not the guy directing the big, fat band.

Cone

No, not the cone of silence like on *Get Smart*. God, don't we wish that was real.

Those damn orange things you hate.

Or:

Those wonderful things that warn you not to run over my ass in the street.

Corporate Commission Complaint

When a customer has gotten so irate over not having service that it's been escalated to the (state government) Corporation Commission. This is when your supervisor walks into the crew room at 6:30 on a Friday night and asks for volunteers to handle said complaint, and suddenly it's a bug-eyed standoff in the crew room, and no one is breathing much less volunteering.

Crawl Space

The area under your house that most of you do not know how to get into so you could figure out, "What the hell is that smell?"
Or:
The area under your house that I HAD to go into to find out your now deceased cat thought the telephone wire was a great chew toy. THAT is what the smell has been for the past year.

Crossed Pair/Hears Others On Line (HOOL)

One side of a cable pair is touching one side of another cable pair. When the two customers whose telephones numbers are on these two cable pairs are talking on them at the same time, they will be able to hear, and sometimes talk to, each other. And we don't charge extra for this! Oddly enough, this is not something people are willing to tolerate for very long, even if it's free.

Cross Box (or SAC Box)

The great big steel box-monolith at the corner of your property that a phone truck parks at for hours and hours at a time. These boxes are the interconnection point of the main cable from the central office and the secondary cables that spider-web out through your neighborhood. While you are thinking, "WTF are they doing all day?" we are arguing with other departments at the telco as to who and how did your service get so screwed up.

I guarantee we spend an obscene amount of time talking to ourselves.

Cutting Out
This is when you are up on a pole, say 25 feet in the air, and the little two-inch spike that they lied about when they said it would keep your ass aloft comes out of the pole, and you suddenly find yourself at ground level in a split second, with a frightening amount of splinters in your forearms and somehow under both your bra cups.

Dial Tone
On a landline, it is an audible tone imposed on the phone line so as to inform to you, when you pick up the receiver, that the circuit is ready for you to begin dialing the desired number.

Dial-Up
Slang term for internet service using "baud rate" modems that function across analog landlines. These were pre-broadband (ADSL) circuits.

D-Rings
A nail attached to a "D" shaped, curved, stiff wire that is used to suspend prem-wire and small drop wires or cables along the surface of homes, buildings, and utility poles.

Preferred method to hang your favorite holiday decor.

Drop (Drop Wire)
The cable that connects your premise interface box to the telco terminal.
Types: aerial, buried, underground, ribbon, temporary, flat, twisted.
Also used for clotheslines, bird parties, and home-made zip-lines.

Drop Clamp
Clamp used to secure the drop cable to the premise as well as to the terminal connection point.
Also see *First Attachment, P-clamp, J-hook, Riser clamp.*

Exchange
Think big-ass network of wires strung along thousands of poles feeding fifty to one hundred thousand businesses and homes in your neighborhood.

First Attachment
The first contact point on your building that the phone drop (cable/wire) is suspended to. Shaped like a goat head, it is often referred to as such.

Gaffed Out Pole
A very old, typically inner-city located, utility pole that has been climbed by techs wearing gaffs so often that the surface looks like a very rough, splintered area that has no clean contact for the gaffs to stab into. Rather hazardous. It is why we carry ladders.

Gauge

Term for outside diameter of the wire (i.e.; 6ga, 12ga, 24ga) or the gun your dumb-ass forgot to lock up before we came to your house to work.

Or: Testing tools used to meter liquid or vapor types of natural gases (i.e.: oxygen, nitrogen).

Ground

A copper and/or steel wire, mesh strap, or thin gauge solid sheet metal strap used to connect a path of continuity from the earth herself to every single area where there is a terminal, cable run, premise interface device, phone pole mountings, and anywhere else where low or high voltage electrical or electronic activity is active. The ground must always be in place as a safety precaution to capture and dissipate stray voltage. Think of it as a dog leash for escaping power. If you disconnect the ground wire from the interface, you can use it for an actual dog leash.

Grounded/Ground

One side of the phone line is touching a ground source. This will put a very loud hum on the line that is impossible to talk over. But you, dear reader, will still try.

Hard Hat

That stupid looking plastic hat we wear to keep shit from cracking our skull.

Subcontractors are much more fashion conscious than we are. They know better than to wear a hard hat every time they work aloft.

They're too smart to get hit in the head when climbing a pole through trees or when in an extended bucket truck working near high-voltage power lines as their work partner drives the truck on the wrong side of the road with NO safety signaling whatsoever to the public.

Man, I should have gone to work for those guys. Would have saved me a lot of bad hair days.

Hard-Wired
Term for connecting a wire to a connection block that is screwed down permanently as opposed to being plugged into like an electrical outlet or a modular (plug type) phone jack.

High Speed
Fast as opposed to slow. Dial-up is a very slow digital circuit as opposed to broadband circuits on fiber or ADSL/VRAD.

Hooks (or Gaffs)

Footgear that is strapped to the lower leg and boots. The upper section is a leather wide-faced pad that has a small belt to wrap around the upper calf area. On the inside leg area and the under-foot/arch area is a J-shaped, steel bar with a 2-inch long steel spike pointing out and downward from the inside foot arch. Another small belt wraps around this lower leg area so as to secure the gaff-spike tightly. Yeah, then we stab that spike into the pole about every 8-12 inches and act like these are tiny little stair steps and climb the pole like a stiff-looking chimpanzee. You know you want to try this. See *Cutting out*.

House Siding Descriptions

Stucco: Looks like freeze-dried oatmeal, this is technically defined as THE WORST FUCKING MATERIAL EVER to use as siding.

Vinyl: Easy to drill through, easy to attach siding clips, makes for a clean wire run.

Wood: See above, vinyl, but with staples

Asbestos: Yep, asbestos. This was akin to drilling through a piece of plate glass with a dull drill bit. Your chances for shattering the entire piece of asbestos were 100%. The only variation was how many pieces it would explode into. And here's the fun part, kids: once you broke the piece of asbestos siding, there was no way to replace it. Because, well, IT'S FUCKING ASBESTOS, PEOPLE, and we finally figured out it can kill us.

Interface

The primary (first) conductor connection point at any premise.

Possibly a new online dating site for geeks.

Internet

That global communication network that has statistically proven that videos of kittens are the most important thing on the planet.

Jack (Port, Outlet)

Any plug-in point used to connect a phone or computer network.

J-Hook

Galvanized steel spike that is one-half inch in diameter by five inches long. One end is tapered like a nail, and the other end is flat like a nail head. At this flat end is an extending j-shaped portion of the spike. This spike is hammered into a wooden pole approximately two and one-half inches. The "j" part is used to attach the drop-wire clamp similar to how a clothes hanger functions.

Lightning Arrestor

When a power surge occurs, such as a power company malfunction or a lightning hit, the arrestor severs the continuity of the wire path to the home or business and redirects the power spike to the ground wire connection, thus neutralizing the surge. Typically, the arrestor will reset after a brief cooldown period. There are times when the arrestor wears out or absorbs a massive power surge and is destroyed. How often do any of these scenarios happen? Every few weeks or days. Bad weather or a clear beautiful day, it does not matter.

Modem

The dial-up or broadband device that interfaces your computer to the internet circuit.

It is the analog or digital translator to change 01100011 01110101 01110100 01100101 00100000 01101011 01101001 01110100 01110100 01100101 01101110, etc. into cute kitten videos.

Modular

Term to describe the change from hard-wired jacks to a jack you could plug into and from.

No Dial Tone

I know, you'd think this one would be self-explanatory. But it could be anything from a customer left his phone unplugged to an ice storm ripped everything off the north side of the house.

Noisy/Static

That awful crackling noise where you're not sure if the line is still connected but you, dear reader, keep trying to talk over it anyway.

Non-Stepped Pole

A pole that is sans steps. These poles require wearing gaffs or the placement of a ladder to ascend.

(See: Hooks or Gaffs)

Open

One or both sides of the cable pair/circuit/line is open. It's broke. It ain't going past this point.

Pair

Term used to describe conductive circuit wiring. There are two, separately insulated copper wires, twisted together along the pathway. Hence the word "pair."

Party Line

No, we're not talking about cocaine.

This is a line with between two and eight households on it, all sharing one cable pair. Used in rural areas where supplying cable for everyone to have a private line was not fiscally feasible. This required wiring every telephone at each residence (one through eight parties, remember?) differently, and a lot of patience and cooperation on the part of everyone sharing the line.

Pedestal (or "Ped")

Term used for the underground or "buried" cable access locations. This is the terminal where drop-to-cable connections are made. Not to be confused as something to landscape around.

Pole

That 20 or 30 foot stick next to your property.

(See: Blind Alley RANT story)

Premise (or "Prem") Wire

The in-house wiring connecting all the jacks to the interface. The same stuff the dogs and cats like to chew on.

AKA:

"IW" (inside wire),

"JKT" (don't remember what the hell that stood for),

"3-wire (or) cloth-3-wire" (for back in the days of party lines. The 3rd wire was to attach to the ground wire in order to arrange the wires inside the set to determine whose phone rings and how many times to ring so you knew the call was for you.),

"QUAD" (when we started to need 2 pairs of wire to add lights in the phones as well as the popularity of second lines. See *additional line*).

Protector
See *arrestor*.

SAC Box (or Cross Box)
See *Cross box*.

Safety Glasses
It is really easy to poke your eye out. Wear 'em, dumb-ass.

Service Emergency

Due to rain, floods, ice, snow, wind, tornadoes, hurricanes – you get the picture – whenever there is a massive loss of service, a service emergency would be declared.

Also known as, Your-Life-Is-Not-Your-Own-Until-All-Services-Have-Been-Restored.

Short/Short and Ground

A short is when both sides of a cable pair/circuit are touching each other. A short and ground is both. What, you don't remember what a ground is? Look it up!

Splice

Points where any and all types of wiring or cables are connected, or spliced, to extend the range of the network connectivity.

Span

This is the expanse of aerial cable between poles.

Stapler (U-Staples)

Duh, you say. Well, we're special and have a special kind of staple gun. Our staples instead of being flat on top are round at the top. This is so as to not cut through the round wire jacket of the *premise wire*.

Step Pole

These were poles fitted with three-quarter inch diameter, twelve-inch long rod-type spikes. The spikes are miniature versions of an off-set ladder step. The aforementioned *gaffed-out* pole now needs something safe to climb on. So, we retrofit with these steps. I mean, ya can't just swap out 30-foot poles all the time, right?

Strand (Support Strand)

Term for a steel cable that is ⅜ inch to ½ inch in diameter. This cable is strung and stretched to and from all aerial poles. They are pulled so tight that most *spans* (the distance between poles) are almost completely without slack. Basically, as tight as a guitar string. The strand performs three functions: (1) As a supportive aspect of the physical structure; (2) As an integral part of the *ground* (or bonded) continuity; (3) As something to tie together, all the cables, splice cases, and assortment drops and other crap we need to drape over your yard.

Strap Wire

Term for the fancy-pants stainless wire we use to strap (or tie) those fat-ass cables to the *strand.*

Support Strand

I just told you all that shit.

Telephone Test Set/Butt Set/Dumbell

Telephone sets we techs carried on our tool belts to communicate with our test center, business office, central office, customers, etc. To use it, we had to physically connect it to your cable pair/dial tone. Where, if you happened to be in the middle of a conversation, we would never listen in. Ever.

Telephony

Official term for all the shit that has anything to do with all the shit you've been reading about.

Terminal

No, I'm not referring to your or my brand of uniqueness. The terminal is the connection point where your drop wire and the main cable connect to each other. Terminals are on the pole, in the ground, in the alley (in air or on ground), in the apartment building basement, in a closet behind a huge stack of crap, behind a secret wall, right next to your desk at work, hidden in the attic, covered up by your landscaper who is convinced that the blind alley utility easement is part of your property. Oh, wait ... that was YOU that covered up MY terminal and then cut the fucking drop with the DIY backhoe you rented and then knew for certain that you did not need to call for a utility locate because you are completely convinced of where that underground cable is placed. Yeah ...

Terminal Room

Refer to the above tirade. This room, I must point out, is sometimes located IN THE MEN'S BATHROOM. Granted, there were only men doing this job when these buildings were built. I did cause a few guys to spray indiscriminately when they heard me say 'woman in the men's room' from INSIDE THE MEN'S ROOM.

Test OK

If you're a lazy technician or the test center, this is when you write off the trouble ticket without even going out to the customer's premise, thereby pissing them off even more.

A test ok usually meant it was intermittent trouble – it wasn't working when the customer reported it, but now it's cleared up. So, if the trouble was caused by rain getting an exposed wire wet, and we wrote it off because now it's dried up in the meantime, guess what happens next time it rains? See Corporate Commission Complaint.

Underground

Manholes. We would have called them she-holes or asshole but one is misogynistic and the other one is, well, bad in mixed company. Wait ... what should we call them now? Submit your suggestion. It might make it into the next volume of random tirades. Anyway ... The Underground is a magical land of hidden things you cannot imagine need to exist, so you can make phone calls, surf the net, or watch your favorite adult cartoon.

Witching

Duh, it's magic.
Shel will attempt to explain. I'm wore out from the, "I don't need no stinking locate" customer.

Witching, rhymes with bitching
When a technician uses two approximately 14-inch long L-shaped pieces of copper wiring, preferably 10-gauge, to locate an underground cable. When said technician (who herself possesses the above-mentioned magic) crosses over the underground cable in question, both L-shaped rods being loosely held in tech's hands will swing towards each other to form a parallel line directly over the underground cable. This is consistently accurate, as I've cross-checked it with an actual locator machine to verify my amazing powers.

GLOSSARY FINAL NOTE

If we forgot something regarding the "Glossary," well, search for it on the "Internet." Ya'know, that thing we installed in your house, so you could access "information."

Feel free to bitch moan and complain about anything we wrote or did not write. We will feel free to pay attention to any of that or not.

MOST OF ALL ... Thank you. For your support, now on this project, and THEN, when we were working to serve YOU and support ourselves.

ABOUT THE AUTHORS

SHELLEY STAIB

Even as a little kid I think I've always been 'out of the box' as far as convention goes. I remember I wanted to be a cowboy, and by the age of five, I was packing a pair of six-shooter cap pistols on a holster I had slung around my hips. I would practice drawing in front of a mirror, and, to this day, I can twirl a cap pistol both forward and backward on my finger and holster it in one smooth move. And, hell yes, I will show you if you doubt me.

My Tonka dump truck was one of my favorite toys, and it was still made of metal back then, like God intended child's toys to be made. Yes, it could be harmful, but so can life.

I was always curious about how stuff worked and what would happen if _____? Like that time when me and my brothers tied some twine to a fence post next to our house, then laid it out across the street to our neighbor's house where we pulled it taut and tied it onto some fixed object. It was about four and a half or five feet above ground level and tight as a banjo string. All we had to do now was wait for a car to come by.

You know what happens when a car going twenty-five mph encounters a piece of twine stretched across the street?

The antenna was sliced off that car like a hot knife through butter! We scattered like cockroaches, and then mom got out the hairbrush that night for a little old-fashioned discipline.

Fifteen years later, I would remember the antenna incident when I didn't have a hacksaw to cut through a plastic PVC pipe I was using for a conduit. I did, however, have some twine. I used that twine and friction to cut the pipe. It's then I realized I've been preparing for this job, and this book, all my life.

Prior to working for Ma Bell, I worked at a local drive-in where I did food prep and worked backup (think fries and tater tots) on the grill. By food prep, I mean I made about six million onion rings, and I am talking carry the fifty-pound bag inside, peel, core and slice them, dip them in water, flour, secret coating mix, and then the final batter and stack them on trays to dry. All. Day. Every. Saturday.

They were damned good onion rings, too. Not the crap they serve today.

I worked on a maintenance crew at an apartment complex where I learned that if I never touch another Rototiller again in my life it will be too soon.

I used my house and everything in it as a training ground for how to repair or replace anything I could take apart. From small plumbing jobs to electrical work, repairing my lawn mower (Yes, it ran, but was it safe? Let's just say I didn't let anyone else use it), and if someone asked me if I could do something, I usually said 'yes' first and then figured out how the hell I was going to do it later.

Along the way, my siblings began procreating, and I found that I had a flair for telling my nieces and nephews stories. Or, more accurately, extravagant and blatant lies, which I made sound very believable. They were so believable, in fact, that only recently have I revealed to the kids that a certain story I've told them for years did not actually happen at all. I was thrilled at their disappointment when they discovered this because it meant I was a damn good storyteller! Nevermind their disillusionment; that's what therapy is for.

As good as my made-up stories were, the stories in this book are all completely true. Seriously, I could not make this stuff up. My natural curiosity about how things work, and can I fix them when they aren't working has served me well during my career at Ma Bell. Yes, this book is about what it was like working for the telephone company. It's also about life. Our human connection. The not-so-little things that happen every day that I have had the privilege to observe and write about. It's about an eighteen-year-old kid who grew up on the job.

I've been telling these stories to my family and friends for years now. I am grateful for the opportunity to share them with you, and I hope you enjoy reading them as much as I enjoyed living them.

CHRISTOPHER GULICK

I suppose my lifelong career as a professional "barnyard engineer" started as a small child.

When your family of origin is not affluent, yet has affluent taste and educational experience, you are taught how to act, speak, behave, and look like you might have said affluent-ness.

That stated, you also develop a tolerance for not really caring on any given day, blowing off the housework for the day, putting on a crappy t-shirt, a ripped pair of jeans, and walking to work because the mechanic has the limo in the shop. That means Dad is at work at the second job and can't fix mom's station wagon this weekend.

Oh, me and/or my brother could have fixed the car, but... our modifications were not always to her liking.

My training in run-what-you-brung and do-with-what-you-have has served me well in my personal life and the myriad of jobs I engaged in prior to the telco tech gig.

Many folks have used derogatory or even blatant tribal slurs to describe the manner of working regarding the aforementioned.

Me? I call it Barnyard Engineering. Common sense is, indeed, NOT common.

I problem-solved as well as modified in some manner most everything I ever touched. At the very least, I left my mark in some minor fashion.

My teen years were a litany of jobs that required this unique engineering mindset.
I remodeled/modified my bedroom in the house of my family of origin.
I was a busboy/dishwasher for a locally-owned restaurant empire.
They required everyone to think fast on their feet. I worked loading delivery trucks at a regional soda-pop bottling plant. I delivered newspapers back before all the adults with cars took those jobs.

While those teen jobs sound like no-brainer menial labor, they had their challenges in a moment-to-moment basis that required abstract thinking regarding how to change to this, when to adjust to that, what is the best thing for right now, and how to accommodate that customer who is completely different than the one before.

Yes, we all have to learn these things, these "simple" things.

Yet, daily, aren't you unpleasantly surprised by how UN-common these skills sets are in fellow humans?

No, it will not get better. Just ask Socrates.

Nonetheless, I enjoyed working inside, outside, and bouncing back and forth. I loved meeting and interacting with new people every day and being privy to the delightful as well as horribly frustrating sets of experiences that accompany such.

My perspectives on their experiences, their moment in time, the locations, the weather, and the characters are what are unique, what are truly mine.

Many of you have and or will have similar dynamics yet will have your own perspective.

You and I are here to relate to one another, not compare our experiences. Take what you can use and leave the rest.

SPECIAL THANKS FROM AUTHORS
AND OTHER ACKNOWLEDGEMENTS

Chris' special thanks:

Special thanks to "Pit", "Fred" and 1123.

The Twilight Zone, God's Country, White-Hell, Am-Worst, Disgusta, Bend-Over, The Animal Farm, Furley, the Valley, Sure-Won't, The Temple of Doom, Jackson-Hole, Murray, PECK(er), and, And-Over-And-Over.

You all gave me a life I am proud to have been a part of, and ... you helped me grow up in public.

Shelley's special thanks:

Special thanks to my family and friends for listening to my stories all these years and for encouraging me to share them.

Made in the USA
Columbia, SC
21 November 2018